Praise for

Legend of the Rainbow Warriors

and other works by Steven McFadden

"This is a great book."

— *Network of Light*

"In this wonderful new book, Steven McFadden manages to weave together the commonality of many divergent legends, myths and sacred teachings. If you're looking for guideposts to light your way, this book is just the thing for you."

— Celeste Longacre
Sweet Fern magazine

Profiles in Wisdom

"If you haven't yet encountered the richness and diversity of the Native American wisdom traditions, read this book. It will open your eyes, and your heart as well. In their own words, seventeen Native elders from throughout the Americas, from Peru to Canada, generously share collective Earth Wisdom gleaned over the millennia. How desperately we need these teachings now."

— Stephen Bodian
editor of *Yoga Journal*

"This is one of those books , once you've read it you will wonder what you had been thinking of the world before that time. It is informative, inspirational, wise and genuinely important."

— Libbi Armati
Amazon.com Reviewer

"*Profiles in Wisdom* does a fine job not only of presenting the dignity, complexity, and wit of important Indian philosophers and religious leaders, but also of issuing cautions against easy uplift and wisdom injections. There are some stirring and unexpected powers unleashed in this book."

— *New York Times Book Review*

"The wide–ranging, informal essays in this book engagingly illuminate many facets of different tribal traditions."

— *Small Press Book Review*

"There is such a wealth and variety of subjects covered in this book that I can't distill it into a few lines. The profiles and photographs of each person are done with such directness and integrity. This would be a valuable book to own for further reference."

— **Sue Dean**
Amerrikua Magazine

"A sensitive and thoughtful job. This unusual book touches on many subjects—mysticism vs. science, the ultimate fate of the Earth, the sacred roles of women and men, the power of primitive medicine, and the connectedness of everything that is of the earth. It can be seen as a blueprint for survival."

— **John W. Maxson**
The Keene Sentinel (Keene, NH)

Legend of the Rainbow Warriors

Legend of the Rainbow Warriors

STEVEN McFADDEN

Invocation by Ven. Dhyani Ywahoo

Chiron Communications
Santa Fe, New Mexico

Chiron Communications
7 Avenida Vista Grande #195
Santa Fe, NM 87505-9199
www.chiron–communications.com

Book and cover design by Janice St. Marie
Cover photo by Jim Van Gundy
Rainbow Warriors sculpture by Heyoka Merrifield
Author photo on back cover by Carolyn Wright,
    The Photography Studio, Santa Fe, New Mexico

© 2001 by Steven McFadden
ISBN 0-9665234-6-6 2/02

Portions of this book were published in 1989 by Chiron Communications under
the title *The Legend of the Rainbow Warriors*. Portions were published in 1992 by Bear
& Co. of Santa Fe, NM under the title *Ancient Voices, Current Affairs: The Legend of the
Rainbow Warriors*.

The poem "For the Children" which appears in Chapter 9 is by
Gary Snyder, from *Turtle Island*, copyright © 1974 by Gary Snyder.
Reprinted by permission of New Directions Publishing Corp.

Publisher's Cataloging-in-Publication

McFadden, Steven, 1948-
    Legend of the rainbow warriors / by Steven McFadden ;
    invocation by Dhyani Ywahoo. --1st ed.--
    p. cm. : ill.
    Includes bibliographical references.
    ISBN 0-9665234-6-6

    1. New Age movement. 2. Civilization, Modern--1950-
--Miscellanea. 3. Indians of North America--Religion--
Miscellanea. 4. Mythology--Miscellanea. 5. Human
ecology--Religious aspects--Miscellanea. I. Title.

BP605.N48M34 2001   291.1'78362
                    QBI01-700419

With love to
Carolyn Clay Mercer-McFadden, Ph.D.
Woman with Many Fires
(1941–1999)

And for all our relations,
especially our godchildren

Contents

Illustrations

Photos

Acknowledgments

I offer my thanks and appreciation to the elders, living and in spirit, who gave voice to the visions which collectively represent what I have come to call the legend of the rainbow warriors and which serve as the basis of this book.

Many friends and acquaintances have made this book possible by contributing inspiration, support and teachings. Among the many helpers are my loving wife Carolyn, now in spirit. Also my family, Lane Badger, Mark Lerner, Jose Arguelles, Medicine Story and Ellika Linden, Slow Turtle, Burne, Wounded Bear, Carole Bedrosian, Marcia Starck, Satyena Ananda, Jonathan and Karen Goldman, Kelley Hunter, Nick Michael, Helyn Connerr, Tomiki, Corinne McLaughlin, Gordon Davidson, Tom Cratsley, the Watkinson family, Betsy Stang and Jim Davis, John Harvey and Lourdes Gray, Juan Salazar, Linda Aranda, John S. Mercer, LaurieJoy Pinkham and Will, Carol Dubois, Paula Cercel, Becky Mulkern, Bryan Field, Betsey Browne, Pauline Zimmer, Brooke Medicine Eagle, Arthur and Marilyn Perkins, Brant Secunda, Bearheart, Garrick Beck, Janice St. Marie, Joe Mowrey, Adrien Gordon, Andrew Elliot, Bob and Celeste Longacre, Ven.Dhyani Ywahoo, Jeff Bumbaco, Linda Lindgren, Barbara and Gerry Clow, Sig Longren, Oh Shinnah, The Jennings Family, Jacki Hayward Gauger and family, Rosemary Cathcart, Dorsey Toney, Shabri Red Bird, Gail Vivino, Marilyn Hager Biethan, Barbara Doern Drew, Angela Werneke, Charla and Tarwater, Horse and Mary Thunder, Rachel Claire and many others I have surely neglected to mention.

Invocation

W e stand today on the threshold of a dream, a harvesting of sacred seeds. May Steven McFadden's *Legend of the Rainbow Warriors* reveal to all the present opportunity to transform discord and cultivate the seeds of right relationship.

As nature has its seasonal cycles, so are there also cycles of planetary growth and dissolution. When we consider the myth of the rainbow warriors, we see that the rainbow is a bridge that connects all cultures, and that the greatest warriors only war upon ignorance—their own as well as that of others—by changing the thought patterns of discord and revealing methods of resolution. In these years every human being will feel the deep influence of unconscious patterns rising to the surface of the mind, which are then acted out in national and international activities. What arises is recognition of that which has kept humans separate from the Earth and from one another.

A tone arises as a pulse from the Earth, the Sun, and the center of our Milky Way galaxy. Paying attention to this pulse, or heartbeat, we are able to come again into resonant harmony with the pulse of the Earth and one another. Our personal thoughts and actions contribute to the future yet another note, a fourth note, which creates a chord and is perceived as a field of action. We were taught this is called the Age of Flowers, when the minds of the people return to the understanding of our relationship with all beings and to the significance of cooperative action.

Bioresonance is a word that signifies patterns—the drumbeat of the Earth and our own interaction with that pattern. In healthy systems, our brains, our breath, and the timbre of our voices resonate harmonically with the drumming heartbeat pulse of the Earth. Then as the Earth's pulse is quickened by an influx of energy from the center of the universe, we find that those patterns that have created discord or blocks in the pulsing flow initially appear more chaotic as they seek resolution. Yet with the release of energy potential that was occluded, abundant opportunities arise for growth and realization.

There is a phrase that is used among many of our elders these days: "Remember the original instructions." These original instructions are the patterns encoded within the DNA helix at the core of our genetic makeup. Just as a guitar being tuned in one part of a room sets the strings of a piano in another part of the room to vibrating, so does the tuning of the universe set our minds in motion. Patterns of suffering have been seeded by the dissonance between what is ideal and what is. Movement toward the ideal—including the hopes of all beings—creates pathways of resolution. Within the discord, with careful discernment, the resolution is revealed.

Just as within the curve of an ocean wave there is wind and turbulence, the winds of change are now moving through all beings. This fine-tuning process stirs the pulses and the waves of our thoughts and lives. Within the curve of the wave resides great turbulence, which is also energy potential, so that we as human beings can bring our encoded potential of health and right relationship—part of the original instructions—to fruition.

Considering the waves of change as opportunities, we human beings now have the option to re-create our relationships, to participate in the manifestation of community, government, high art, and service. As this potential becomes more apparent, we see that certain pathways exist through which the forms arise. The first pathway is that of clear intention—that we hold the intention to be in right relationship with our families, our friends, our co-workers, the nations, and the land.

Nations are indeed living organisms, affecting and affected by the environment where they dwell.

Just as an infant recognizes its parents and parents recognize the needs of their child, the innate ability of subtle communication is a path to human survival. As parents recognize a child's needs and respond, a similar dynamic can play out between groups and the environment. The reawakening of this dynamic has the potential to purify the winds and the water. For example, just as energy holds an electron in a neutron's orbit, so do similar fields of energy hold us in relationship with the Earth, to the community, and to one another. The basic resonance, or first tone, is that of family. I interpret my elders' counsel to "remember the original instructions" as being about reawakening those resonant fields of communication that enable us to work in a synergistic way with our families, our friends, our co-workers, our nations, and the living planet herself.

These original instructions are beyond dogma. They are like the cords wrapped around a thread that make a fabric strong, or the overtones of a melody that gives a symphony its cohesiveness. It is no longer a matter of leaders leading us. Rather, we must lead ourselves into right relationships with each other and with the Earth. This will require our cooperative interaction, clear visioning, recognition of the relationships, and developing the skills of reconciliation. The process of healing begins in our own hearts as we consider what it is that we wish to accomplish, how it will benefit our relatives and future generations, and who we will invite to build it with us. The great lesson that humanity is now receiving is the lesson of right relationship. We can no longer relinquish our responsibility, if, indeed, we already have, and it is no longer possible or wise for a few leaders to make decisions for many. We must all participate in the forms arising.

Consider time as moving energy, like the sand in an hourglass. The past, present, and future now fold upon each other, enabling humankind to correct the errors of the past and extract from the collective experience the lessons learned. The millennium is upon us in the form of quickened radiation from the stars, an inpouring of energy through the widening holes in the ozone layer and holes in time—revealing the inconsistency of a worldview that gives humanity the right to dominate the environment, and that sees people as being incongruent with the fields of life. We have learned that the oceans are affected by that which we attempt to cast away, thereby decimating life in the seas. Energy is neither lost nor created. We share in the dance of change; the winds are formed by what we cast aloft. The actions of individuals and nations bear directly upon the present and the future.

All beings who live on Earth have something to contribute to her well being. Governments, including their citizenry, aid the cycle of reciprocity. The ideal of a millennium of peace is with our means. Such technology is now available to invite direct participation of citizens in decision making and planning. Let us remember that we are children of the same mother. While the archetypes of her action are colored by culture and environment, all particulars resolve into the one truth: we are living on Earth.

In the Garden of Eden—the realm of Ongawi as it is known in one native culture—it is understood that the ideal is revealed by the gardener's skill in planting seeds of right relationship. The great peace begins as a seed in our hearts. The dream stirs us all to consider our actions unto future generations. The "how" is revealed in our hoping. Envision, energize with prayerful appreciation; invite all those who have marveled at the beauty of the rainbow to build cooperatively the world of beauty. All the gifts of heaven have long been engraved in our hearts, and now is the time to sweep away confusion and to take note of what is.

VEN. DHYANI YWAHOO
Bristol, Vermont—May, 1992

(Dhyani Ywahoo is founder and spiritual director of the Sunray Meditation Society.)

Prologue

"Throughout the inhabited world, in all times and under every circumstance, the myths of man have flourished; and they have been the living inspiration of whatever else may have appeared out of the activities of the human body and mind. Myth is the secret opening through which the inexhaustible energies of the cosmos pour into human cultural manifestation."

— JOSEPH CAMPBELL

For most of the twentieth century, and even now at the start of the twenty-first, a dominant myth in the developing world has been a version of the American Dream suggesting that most people can attain great wealth and that happiness will follow. However, the promised wealth has never been attainable for millions. Those who have attained the wealth, by and large, may now realize that this part of the dream is hollow. Material riches in and of themselves bring no peace, carry no happiness. Tragically, the unbridled pursuit of this dream, often by people deep in sleep, has plunged us into a nightmare of environmental devastation, ethical bankruptcy, and cultural confusion. Meanwhile, many contemporary observers predict that ethnic conflict and the scarcity of clean water will be the prime causes of war in the twenty-first century.

Perhaps even more passionately than our ancestors, we yearn for a dream that can unify us and direct us again in a good way. We seem to have lost it all: our tribe, our extended families, and our geographic, linguistic, and cultural roots. Where are we in this New World we call America? What have we made of our lives together?

For the most part, we live in a high-speed, high-tech, electronically stimulated world of abstraction. The threats of nuclear or environmental annihilation hang—for the most part unseen—over each moment. While there is material wealth for some, there is spiritual poverty for most. In a sense, all this is the result of myth gone awry.

As we cast about for meaning and direction, two venerable and related myths have begun to emerge: the myth of a new age and the Legend of the Rainbow Warriors. Though widely disparaged, the myth of a new age echoes an ancient theme in storytelling: paradise lost, paradise regained. We have lost paradise in our modern world. Is it therefore surprising that there should arise in our epoch many hopeful myths of a new age, a time when paradise may be regained?

As we move into a new millennium, many storytellers are animating these emerging myths with their words, their art, and their music. Rainbows are steadily firing the imaginations of many millions of people. But will these myths penetrate world culture sufficiently to make a positive difference? That is a question only historians will be able to answer.

This book seeks to further clarify the emerging myth of the rainbow, and to demonstrate its living connection to the news unfolding each night on the television screen. The technique for telling this story is a blend of journalism and mythic storytelling. Through journalism, I have gathered critical news stories and sought to establish how seemingly unrelated events can have a deep connection. Through myth I have taken the process a step further and offered an explanation, or meaning, for the events—thereby striving to link ancient voices with current affairs. This technique might well be called mythojournalism.

The various stories in this book are, in fact, one. Together they tell a saga that is larger than the sum of their collective parts. The thread that links them is the legend of the rainbow warriors; part, I feel, of the emerging myth of a New Age. In brief, the Legend of the Rainbow Warriors says that when the Earth becomes desperately sick through the doings of human beings, some of the people will recognize that they are steadily destroying themselves and their Earth Mother. With spiritual insight and support, the Rainbow Warriors—people of all colors and faiths—will come to the rescue, eventually establishing a long and joyous reign of peace.

As I hear it, this modern myth suggests there will be no one hero in this time, no George Washington or Joan of Arc to rescue us from the great dilemma we have created. We must do it ourselves. In that sense, the legend of the rainbow warriors is, to use a modern term, a holistic myth, wherein we all have both the opportunity and the responsibility to become spiritually awakened heroes.

The overall myth points out the general direction that we need to travel: a direction in which there is full respect for the self, for others, and for all the creations who share life with us upon the Earth. By proceeding in this direction, we will create a spiritually informed culture that uses scientific technology to maintain freedom and enhance the balance of life. From that perspective, this book is a journalist's dispatch on how the myth of a New Age is unfolding in the world.

The news events reported within the context of the rainbow prophecies are all true. You can flip open *Facts on File* and verify them; they are the stuff of daily news stories from *The New York Times, The Boston Globe,* CBS, and other standard sources. Does this mean that there is a direct connection between them and the myth, and that the legends and prophecies are true? Who can say with certainty? I know only that people need myth in their lives and that, as myth, the rainbow legends have inspired me and helped give meaning to the chaos of the times. I have also seen how the stories inspire and uplift others when I share them in gatherings both large and small. This gives me hope.

For these many reasons, I offer this volume: to clarify the myth, to explore its connection to present reality, and to inspire people to work toward making the dream real by engaging in an ancient quest: seeking practical ways to bring heaven to Earth.

As Joseph Campbell suggested in his writings, ultimately it matters little whether a myth is based on ascertainable fact or not. What matters is whether the myth helps people to live better, more satisfying lives— not just for themselves alone, but as part of a community, as part of the fabric of life on this planet. In this way, if people choose it out of their intelligence and free will, a myth that has been unreal can become real.

Chapter One

Legend of the Rainbow Warriors

I n the spring of 1983 I met a handsome young woman named Brooke Medicine Eagle. She was standing in a circle of people on a wooded knoll near the Hudson River on the East coast of Turtle Island (North America). Brooke was striking a drum rhythmically to match the silent but all-pervading heartbeat of the Earth Mother. She asked all of the people in the circle to acknowledge the heartbeat of the Earth as something they shared in common, and then she told the story of her vision.

Brooke is a metis, a woman of Crow and Sioux heritage. As she stood on the knoll, she told how, in preparation for her work as a healer, she had purified herself in a sweat lodge and then climbed to the summit of Bear Butte in South Dakota. There she fasted for four days and nights, crying out to the Great Mystery for a vision to guide her.

In time, as the moon began to rise and a rainbow marked half the twilit sky, a holy woman dressed in buckskin appeared and stood next to her. Moonbeams shone upon the woman, revealing each particle of the buckskin dress as a rainbow unto itself with the full sparkling spectrum. Then a vision unfolded. A double circle of friends and teachers appeared, and began to dance in a sacred manner around Brooke and the woman.

PHOTO 1. *Brooke Medicine Eagle. Photo by Jaime S. Brittain, Illuminessence, ©2000.*

Then the spirit woman began to convey energy to Brooke through her solar plexus. Some of that energy Brooke sensed physically, some emotionally, some intellectually.

Much of what was communicated to her, Brooke later said, she did not fully understand. But she was able to grasp a part of the message, and that is what she shared with us in 1983. She said her vision revealed what is obvious to those who look upon the world with an open heart: we are living in a time of great change. As a result of human action, much of the world is desperately out of balance. In this time of great change, we can destroy our world or we can heal it. For healing to come about, we need to honor the spirit within ourselves and within all things. We must remember that the Earth is our Mother, and we must take care of her; we must remember that we are all related, and we must respect all the things that make life possible.

After telling her vision, Brooke—whose sacred name is Daughter of the Rainbow of the Morning Star Clan Whose Helpers Are the Sun and the Moon and Whose Medicine Is the Eagle—turned to look at the people who encircled her. She told how, for several days after her vision, she saw rainbows in the sky again and again. During those days she began to understand more of her vision. "We have the opportunity to build a rainbow bridge into a Golden Age," she explained. "But to do this we must do it together with all the colors of the rainbow, with all the peoples, all the beings of the world. We who are alive on Earth today are the Rainbow Warriors who face the challenge of building this bridge."

As I listened to Brooke tell her story, I was entranced. Her powerful presence and dramatic story touched some remote part of me, as if I had heard the story before in childhood, or dreamed a similar dream. I wanted to understand more.

In the weeks and months that followed, I set time aside for reading and meditating on the rainbow. I learned that the rainbow theme is sounded frequently in the dreams and visions of the holy men and women of the Native American tradition, as well as in Australia and Tibet. The myth of the rainbow encompasses far more than the story of a lone Ark adrift for 40 days and nights.

The rainbow story is told many ways and in many different places around the world, including on Turtle Island—from the southlands called Mexico, to the heartland called United States, to the northlands now called Canada. It has been told for hundreds of years, from dozens of perspectives. Among the many ancient versions of rainbow visions, I noted in particular the stories of Eyes of Fire of the Cree nation, Black Elk of the Lakota, Crazy Horse of the Oglala, Quetzalcoatl of the Toltec, Plenty Coups of the Crow, Ku'Kulkan of the Maya, Monteczuma of the Aztec, the Peacemaker of the Iroquois Six Nations, Weetucks of the Wampanoag, and several others. Though they lived at different times and in different places, they shared a sense of what might come.

The Legend

In brief, in amalgamated form, here is the Legend of the Rainbow Warriors as described in times past by American Indian visionaries, who glimpsed with foresight the arrival of light-skinned people on Turtle Island (North America).

> Light-skinned people will come out of the eastern sea in great canoes powered by huge white wings, like giant birds. The people who get off these boats will also be like birds, but they will have two different kinds of feet. One of their feet will be like that of a dove, the other like that of an eagle. The foot of the dove will represent a beautiful, new religion of love and kindness, and the foot of the eagle will represent strength, technology, and power. The sharp foot of the eagle will dominate, for though they will talk much of the new religion, not all of the light-skinned people will live by it. Instead they will claw at the Red Nations with their eagle feet, exploiting and enslaving them.

After offering mixed resistance to this clawing, the Indians would seemingly lose their spirit and be herded into small, barren enclaves. This would be the way of their world for many years: poverty, suffering, disrespect. Then in time the world would become sick. Because of unrelenting greed, the Earth would be filled with deadly liquids and metals, the air would be rendered foul with smoke and ash, and even the rains—which are intended to cleanse the Earth—would plummet in poison drops. Birds would fall from the sky. Fish would turn belly up in the waters. Forests would begin to wither. There would be mounting chaos—*koyanisquatsi*—in the world.

When these things begin to happen, the Indian people would be all but helpless. But then Light would come from the East, and the natives would begin to find their strength, their pride, and their wisdom. So would many of their brothers and sisters of the other nations—white, yellow and black—who would feel strongly the calling of Spirit. They would understand the basic fact that it is the Earth which gives us the water, food, clothing, shelter and beauty necessary for the circle of life. These awakened souls would find each other, and together they would teach all the people of the world to have respect for the Earth Mother, of whose very stuff human beings are made. Respect would prevail.

Under the symbol of the rainbow all the races and religions would band together to spread the great wisdom of living in harmony with each other and with all the creations of the world—and thereby restore the Sacred Hoop. Those who teach this way would be the Warriors of the Rainbow, but they would do no harm. Using peaceful means alone, and by becoming examples of right living, after a great struggle they would bring an end to the destruction and desecration of the Earth.

The tasks of rainbow warriors would be many and great. There would be mountains of ignorance to conquer and they would meet prejudice and hatred. They must be dedicated, unwavering in strength, and strong of heart. They would find willing hearts and minds that would follow them on this road of healing. Peace and plenty would then reign through a long and joyous Golden Age.

As I researched, I absorbed all of these new ideas with great attention. The story haunted me, gnawed at me, and finally, in combination with other forces on my path, drew me into the forests and then onto a mountain summit alone, in search of a more complete understanding.

In the forests and on the mountains I was gifted with insight. I learned the way of the four directions and heard the message of the winged ones, the birds. In deep peace on a northern New England summit, I saw in sharp relief how modern times and the myth were echoes of each other. I resolved to tell the story.

Months passed. I went with my wife Carolyn to Provincetown, Massachusetts to rest by the sea. There—amidst the posters, bumper stickers, and people in a Greenpeace gift shop—I had another revelation. I saw and felt how deeply others had been influenced by the rainbow vision.

When the founders of Greenpeace heard the rainbow legend they were far out at sea, already working for a measure of sanity in a world dizzy for material gain. The rainbow impressed them so forcefully that they named Greenpeace's first and foremost ship the Rainbow Warrior. The ship became a focal point for inspiration and action, a vehicle through which human beings could assert themselves on behalf of their Earth Mother.

From this feeling of connection with the legend and with Greenpeace, I drew hope and inspiration. I walked my own part of the rainbow path for two and a half years while Brooke Medicine Eagle walked her part, studying the lessons that life drew to her. Then Brooke came east for a week, calling another circle of people together near the murky waters of the Charles River in Massachusetts.

When the people arrived and joined in this circle, Brooke took a moment to find her balance. Then she leaned back and opened herself to the Divine, what she called Great Mystery. With song and story, she sounded the new tone that she hears being set in the world: a tone of the heart, of healing, and of harmony. We all breathed in balance, and then we sang and danced in a sacred manner.

Brooke told again of her personal glimpse of the rainbow vision. She addressed the circle of people using a common rhetorical device.

"I've got some good news and some bad news," she said. "The good news is that those of us who hear these things and feel them deeply are the Warriors of the Rainbow. We are here now to take on the challenge of building a rainbow bridge into a time that works for everyone and everything that makes life possible. The bad news is that we must do it today. The time of waiting is over. The Earth changes have begun, and we are called to heal the world."

When I heard Brooke say these things the second time, by the banks of the Charles River, they no longer sent me off into a dreamy void. By that time I had already been to a craggy summit in the far North to seek another vision. There I had seen a star-filled sky, eight rainbows ringing the horizon, and an eagle on the wing higher than I had ever imagined a creature of flesh and blood might reach. Vision had come, along with deeper insight. I had spoken with the rainbow and had come to know that the rainbow path was growing wider. I had

FIGURE 1. *The Author's Vision. Eight rainbows ringed the horizon, and an eagle lifted up on wing and soared above. (illustration by Marilyn Hager Biethan).*

seen that the many brothers and sisters who walked these pathways were growing in strength and skillful means. On that mountain my own heart filled with peace. Later, as I stood in a circle with Brooke and twenty-five other sisters and brothers, that peace became a power in the world.

Chapter Two

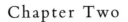

Counsel
of the Elders

A s there are many colors in the rainbow, so there are many versions of the rainbow legend on Turtle Island—the vast land mass ranging from the northlands we know as Canada, to the southlands we call Central America. All versions of the legend sound the themes of respect for the Earth, respect for the plants and animals that make our lives possible, and respect for ourselves and others across the spectrum of viewpoints and colors: red, white, brown, yellow, and black.

The legends also sound the theme of unity through diversity. Thomas Banyacya, an elder of the Hopi Nation, once observed that "as Native Americans, we believe the rainbow is a sign from the Spirit in all things. It is a sign of the union of all peoples, like one big family. The unity of all humanity—many tribes and peoples—is essential."

Hopi people have many engaging and thought–provoking stories to tell about Turtle Island, and and the role of native people in con-tributing their practical and spiritual insights to modern culture. Other native groups hold complementary mythic elements. As reported by Vinson Brown in *Voices of the Earth and Sky*, around 1871 the great chief of the Teton Sioux, Crazy Horse, had a powerful vision that clearly sounded the rainbow theme.

He saw his people being driven into spiritual darkness and poverty while the white people prospered in a material way all around them. But even in the darkest times he saw that the eyes of a few of his people kept the light of dawn and the wisdom of the Earth, which they passed on to some of their grandchildren. He saw the coming of automobiles and airplanes and twice he saw great darkness and heard screams and explosions when millions died in two great world wars.

But after the second great war passed, he saw a time come when his people began to awaken, not all at once, but a few here and there, and then more and more. He saw that they were dancing in the beautiful light of the Spirit World under the Sacred Tree even while still on Earth. Then he was amazed to see that dancing under that tree were representatives of all races who had become brothers, and he realized that the world would be made new again and in peace and harmony, not just by his people, but by members of all the races of humankind.

Many contemporary native leaders also offer insight on the teachings of the rainbow. Together, their insights add depth and color. Many of the elders who were subjects for my related book, *Profiles in Wisdom: Native Elders Speak about the Earth*, offered views of the rainbow. The rainbow teachings were widely dispersed in that book, but in this chapter the teachings are consolidated so they may be seen plainly.

Seven Prophets, Seven Fires

Grandfather William Commanda of the Mamuwinini, one of the Algonquin nations, is a wisdom keeper of the North. All his life he has lived on the Kitigan Zibi Indian Reserve in Maniwaki, Quebec, where he has been a hunting guide, canoe maker, and a forestry worker. Grandfather Commanda is the Keeper of the Primstaven, a carved wooden staff given to the Indian people by the Vikings about a thousand years ago. The carvings on the staff convey the teachings and prophecies of the Viking people. In essence, these prophecies assert that although different people have different ways of understanding, there is only one Creator. All people, no matter their color or their religious traditions, come from this Creator. Some day, as the carvings on the stick

Photo 2. Grandfather William Commanda. Author photo.

represent, all people will recognize and honor this basic truth.

In addition to the Primstaven, Grandfather Commanda is keeper of the Seven Fires wampum belt, which was fashioned in the 1400s out of beads from quahog clam shells (*poquauhock* in Algonquin) and sinew. The long, thin beads are either creamy white, or a soft, mystical lavender color. Using diamond-shaped symbols formed from the beads, this belt symbolically tells how seven prophets came before the Algonquin people many years ago.

The seven prophets took turns, and spoke of seven epochs of history to come, called the Seven Fires. As interpreted by contemporary Native elders, including Eddie Benton Banai of the Midewiwin Lodge and William Commanda, it is understood that the markings on the wampum belt convey a long story of migration and momentous events.

During the time of the Fourth Fire, the prophets said, a light-skinned people would come to Turtle Island, the home of the Red Nations, and things would change. "If the light-skinned race comes in brotherhood and without weapons," the prophets declared, "then there will come a time of wonderful change for generations." But they counseled that if the light-skinned race came wearing the face of death, then the people would have to be careful. The face of brotherhood and the face of death would look similar, but the face of death would soon be revealed in the form of greed for the riches of the land. "You shall know that they wear the face of death," the prophets said, "if the rivers run with poison and the fish become unfit to eat."

In the story represented by the wampum belt, according to the elders, it is said that "in the confusing times of the Sixth Fire a group of visionaries came among the people. They gathered all the priests of the Midewiwin Lodge, and told the priests that the Midewiwin Way was in danger of being destroyed. They gathered all the sacred bundles.

They gathered all the scrolls that recorded the ceremonies. All these things were placed in a hollowed-out log from the Ironwood tree. Men were lowered over a cliff by long ropes. They dug a hole in the cliff and buried the log where no one would find it. Thus, the teachings of the elders were hidden out of sight, but not out of memory. It was said that when the time came that the Indian people could practice their religion without fear, that a little boy would dream where the Ironwood Log, full of sacred bundles and scrolls, was buried. He would lead his people to that place."

The Seventh Fire on the belt—the only one symbolized by a double diamond pattern of beads—offers a promise of hope. According to Grandfather Commanda, the seventh prophet said that in the time of the Seventh Fire a new people would emerge. They would retrace their steps to find the wisdom that was left by the side of the trail long ago. Their steps would take them to the elders, who they would ask to guide them on their journey. "If the new people remain strong in their quest, the sacred drum will again sound its voice. There will be an awakening of the people, and the Sacred Fire will again be lit. At this time, the light-skinned race will be given a choice between two roads. One road is the road of power and technology guided by greed and fear, and lacking wisdom or respect for life. This road represents a rush to ultimate destruction. The other road is spirituality, a slower path that includes respect for all living things. If we choose the spiritual path, we can light yet another fire, an Eighth Fire, and begin an extended period of peace and healthy growth."

Grandfather Commanda understands that we are now in the time of the Seventh Fire and that the choice of the two roads is before us. He prays every day that we will honor the North and make our choice from the place of wisdom, recognizing Light in all the rainbow creations of the world.

Return of the Rainbow People

Sun Bear (Vincent LaDuke) was a Chippewa teacher who traveled the world to share the prophecies of native peoples and to warn of Earth changes. He crossed into spirit on June 20, 1992 in Spokane, Washington.

The originator of the popular Medicine Wheel Gatherings, Sun Bear was a gifted orator, with eloquence, insight, and force. "All the prophecies of the native people speak of a time when the human beings

Photo 3. Sun Bear. Photo courtesy of the Bear Tribe Medicine Society.

will face a choice between going on the same way with greed and technology or going toward Spirit. I feel, and many others feel, that now is that time when we face that choice. We need to go toward Spirit now. These prophecies were given to warn all people on the planet, not just the natives but all the people on the planet. That way they can make the necessary changes in their lives. We have to shift our dependencies back to the Earth and back to each other as human beings. That's the only way we can go.

"For example, the prophecies of the Hopi people foresaw both world wars, and that they would be fought against the sign of the four directions (Germany's Maltese cross, and swastika) and against the sun sign (Japan's rising sun). They foresaw the invention of the automobile, the airplane, even the atom bomb. Native prophets also spoke of a time when the sons of the white men would grow their hair long, wear beads, and live in communal societies. When that time came, according to the old ones, the cleansing would be at hand. It happened in the Sixties with flower power, the anti-Vietnam protestors, the Berkeley Free Speech Movement, and so on.

"Native prophecies say that those mixed-blood and white people who grew their hair long and wore beads would come to Native healers and ask for guidance. Some of these people would be returning spirits of the Indians slaughtered during the conquest of the continent. The prophecies say that they would return as rainbow people in bodies of different colors —red, white, yellow, black—and that they would return and unite to help restore balance to the earth.

"The story of these rainbow warriors is told by many peoples in many different ways. We feel that we are in that time now, when the rainbow warriors are coming about. The human race is no longer at a point where anybody can necessarily hold up their hand and say they are pure this or that. Even among the Indian tribes, you know, they might be all Indian, but they are Indian from two or three different tribal groups. So it's a time when we are having to acknowledge that we are all human beings upon the same planet, and that's what the Rainbow Warriors is all about.

"If you wake up and realize that we are Rainbow Warriors now, that we are a rainbow people upon the Earth, then the next step is becoming a spiritual warrior—someone who is willing to put their energy into something that helps to heal the Earth and restore the balance, and who is interested in doing that consistently, not just showing up for a weekend demonstration, but people who are willing to use their life energy to create a world of balance and harmony for our children after us."

It's the Way You Live Your Life

Oh Shinnah Fastwolf is a warrior woman. In her blood are mixed the traditions of the Tineh (Apache), the Mohawk, and the Scottish. She explains that her work in life, her challenge, is to be a warrior: speaking, singing, and acting on behalf of the Earth. To become recognized as a warrior, she had to go through all of the spiritual, physical, and mental training that Tineh men go through, including the Run for the Sun. That's an eight-to-ten-mile run attempted on the winter solstice. Candidates run the whole way before sunrise with water in their mouths. They must arrive at the Ceremony of the Mountain Spirits at the exact moment of sunrise to contribute their water. Oh Shinnah completed the run when she was eleven, and again at age forty just to prove she could still do it.

As with many indigenous teachers, Oh Shinnah is well aware of the rainbow prophecies. "The prophecies of many native peoples speak of the days of purification. We live them now. In these days we have the opportunity to do something real with our lives. It requires surrender and sacrifice to become a warrior; one must develop a strength so present that one will act, instead of react, always for the good of the whole, regardless of emotional impact. Our lives are short, but each life can make a difference."

Back in the 1970s, Oh Shinnah took part in the Longest Walk, a demonstration in which Indian people walked from California to Washington to protest the many injustices perpetrated against them by

PHOTO 4. *Oh Shinnah Fastwolf. Photo by Michael Silverwise.*

the government. At the end of the walk, some native people angrily confronted her because she was not a full-blooded Native American.

Part of the concern of those who confronted Oh Shinnah was that she was sharing native ceremonies with non-native people, something they felt should not happen. Oh Shinnah responded to them by saying that the wisdom and ceremonies she shares comes from many traditions around the world, and that she teaches very little of the native tradition, and then only what her mentors have given her authority to teach. "I must say I have mixed feelings about non-Indians leading Indian ceremonies. There is a prophecy that states a time would come when Indians would reincarnate on this planet as part of the dominant society, which is white society. The Indians' spirits would incarnate in the dominant society to change the attitude of that society. So learning native ways is very natural to them.

"In this prophecy, these people would wear feathers and beads, and communicate with the flowers. The flowers, it is said, would guide them, and support them as they walked their life paths. Once you learn to communicate with the flowers, you will be led from flower to flower to help you eliminate prejudice and hate from your life. This will also be a time when all the esoteric teachings of the world's traditions will be revealed, so that there will be no secrets, no reason to fear each other or to be in conflict. This is clearly what is happening now.

"Not everyone has the strength or disposition to be a warrior. Many are Rainbow Walkers. They are the people who are walking simply and with dignity from this old time where there is hate and disrespect for the Earth. They are walking across the rainbow bridge to the new time, but they must leave the inconsistencies and the hate behind, or the seeds of hate will be planted in the new time where they will blossom later.

"People are being drawn to native ways because Mother Earth is experiencing trauma and calling to them. Native people are the keepers of Mother Earth. Our original instruction from Great Spirit was to take care of her. If a person has a sincere heart and wants to walk the path of the sacred, it should be accessible to them. The prophecies say we should do this. It is wrong for us not to share our spirituality with those who have lost theirs. But people should be very cautious with traditions they don't understand. People who participate in a ceremony and are not clear about what they are doing can create inharmonious results."

"As far as I'm concerned, it doesn't have anything to do with the color of your skin. It's the way you live your life. The only thing we have to give is the way we live our lives. If you live on this land, and you have ancestors sleeping in this land, I believe that makes you native to this land. It has nothing to do with the color of your skin. I was raised not to look at people racially. What I was taught is that we're flowers in Great Spirit's garden. We share a common root, and the root is Mother Earth. The garden is beautiful because it has different colors in it, and those colors represent different traditions and cultural backgrounds."

New People, New World

For many years Manitonquat (Medicine Story) served as the *powwah*, or spiritual leader, and the *minatou*, or keeper of the lore, for the Assonet band of the Wampanoag Nation. The ancestral land of his people is on the seacoast of Massachusetts. They are the Indians who met the Pilgrims, and who have since antiquity been known as the People of the Morning Light

Manitonquat now works with prison inmates and travels the world to tell his stories, which offer insights about how to live at peace with each other and the natural world. He has had many adventures through his life. One of the greatest of those adventures has been his involvement with a little–known social phenomenon that has happened every summer since the 1970s: the Rainbow Gatherings. Manitonquat has told the story of the gatherings many times.

"In 1972, I went to my first Rainbow Gathering and my life turned all around. Early in that year I received word of a great gathering that was planned to be held in the summer in the Colorado Rocky Mountains. Since it was to be people of all races, religions, nationalities, classes, and lifestyles, it was called a Gathering of the Rainbow Tribes. There was to be a walk, a pilgrimage to Table Mountain, a place sacred

Photo 5. Manitonquat (Medicine Story). Photo by Linda Derman.

to the Arapaho. The people planned to fast and stay in silence all day on that mountain while praying for world peace and understanding.

"Now there are old prophecies that at the end of this world many people of many different nations and tribes would come together to seek a new world and a new way. This would be according to the vision the Creator placed in their hearts. Then, you know, seeing how sincerely they sought this, how deeply they desired it, Great Spirit would hear the cries of their hearts and take pity on them. At that time, the prophecies said, the new world would be born in the midst of the old. This new world would be very small at first, like a newborn baby. But it would be full of life and learning and growth, full of trust and love, like a newborn. Because of this, the new world wouldn't hate the dying old world, but instead learn how to survive and become strong within it. It was said that the sign the Creator would send of this new beginning would be a white buffalo.

"Over 20,000 people came to that first gathering, and everyone was treated with respect. It was wonderful. One night it rained. The next day when we came out in the meadow, we saw that a huge patch of white snow on the side of the mountain that faced us had been eaten away and carved by the rain into the perfect shape of a white buffalo. People began to cheer and sing, and many of them wept joyfully.

"Then starting at Midnight on the third of July everybody began a walk over the eight miles to Table Mountain. All night long that line moved in silence, carrying candles and torches. At dawn thousands of people stood still upon the mountain, people who had come from all over the world to be together and share that moment, to watch the sun rise on a new day, a new people, a new world.

"People stayed together all day on that mountain. We fasted and remained in silence until, sometime after noon, someone started singing an Arapaho chant. All of us took up that chant to honor the traditional caretakers of that land. When we left that gathering everyone had the feeling that something very important had happened, and was happening all over the world. No one could say exactly what it was, or knew what to do about it. So everyone went home and went on with their business. But the next summer a lot of the people decided the only way they could learn what to do with this new energy was to gather again and keep on gathering until the spirit directed something different. That's how it's been. Ever since the Rainbow World Family Gathering of the Tribes has been held during the first week of July."

The dream of the Rainbow Gathering was dreamed after the cultural watershed of Woodstock, when a commune named the Hog Farm and a clown named Wavy Gravy helped feed 400,000 people. That spiritual service was immensely inspiring to the founders of the Rainbow Gathering.

As the founders of the gathering saw it, the rainbow is a sign of the unity of all people in the universal family. And as the fliers for the annual gathering typically proclaim, "the people who gather are a tribe not of blood but of spirit, for all are born into it. We are bound together by our desire to live in peace, to be in the cathedral of nature, and to heal ourselves through union with the earthly mother and the heavenly father. The Rainbow Gathering is an opportunity to celebrate human diversity, to venerate the earth, to deepen connections, and to party—to share a community that is beyond the rules of violence, prejudice, and caste." Each summer the gathering moves to a new state and sets up camp in one of the National Forests. At the gatherings there is no exchange of money. The Rainbow Tribe relies on cooperation, respect, goodwill, and equal rights. For at least one joyful week every summer, it more or less works.

Medicine Story attended the first fifteen Rainbow Gatherings consecutively and is considered one of its grandfathers. He has also attended Rainbow Gatherings in Europe and at the Arctic Circle. As he has matured, the gatherings and the vision they represent have been deeply important to him.

"One reason my life turned around," he explains, "was this vision of twenty thousand people getting together on top of a mountain praying in silence for a new world to be ushered in. The whole thing was so powerful. I knew something was happening. I didn't know what, or how, but I knew I had to be a part of it. Also, I met a number of young Indians who, although they weren't very traditional, came from people who were traditional and had their traditions together. They invited me to their reservation, to the Sun Dance and the Sweat Lodge, and things like that. And so I opened up into a whole world of traditional old ways that I knew little about. Those two things came together at the same time, this rainbow communal world vision, and the old ways, finding that there were still the old ways, and going to seek them out. I kept balancing those two things."

The Rainbow Seeds

The indigenous peoples of the Americas say they have known for many hundreds of years that there were people in all Four Directions and that Indian people long ago visited other places to study and exchange art, science, and other ideas. The native culture of the Americas, though, began to change drastically itself with the coming of Christopher Columbus.

In the South, the tribulation of indigenous people began in earnest when Hernando Cortés arrived in what is now known as Veracruz, Mexico, on Good Friday, AD 1519 with a Roman Catholic priest at his side. The indigenous people say they knew that someone like Cortés would come, and thanks to their elaborate calendars they knew to the exact day when this would happen. They had, in fact, sent scouts to Veracruz to greet Cortés, for they hoped he would be the return of the great spiritual messenger, Quetzalcoatl, whose symbol is the Rainbow Feathered Serpent. Instead, Cortés proved to be the harbinger and the agent of great sorrow.

The Aztec emperor Montezuma II felt his power was threatened. He was frightened by the omens and the legend of Quetzalcoatl, which prophesied the return of that god from the East. He did everything short of violence to prevent Cortés from advancing inland. But Cortés did advance. The rest of the story is one of bloodshed, disease, and trouble as the native people were systematically killed or enslaved.

According to Hunbatz Men, a shaman and daykeeper for the Mayan people of Mexico's Yucatan peninsula, "the problem is that when the

Europeans came to visit they did not respect anything that was already here. The native people could have built more weapons when they became aware that the white men were coming, but the elders knew this was not the path of wisdom. They took another approach."

As reckoned by the elaborate Mayan calendars that Hunbatz has studied his whole life, just as Cortés was stepping ashore, a long cycle of thirteen heavens was coming to an end. For the Maya, it was the beginning of a dark cycle of pain, suffering, sadness and death—the beginning of the reign of *Xibalba*, the world of the Nine Lords of Darkness, the Nine

PHOTO *6. Hunbatz Men. Author photo*

Bolontikus, the Nine Hells. Though in many respects the time of the Nine Hells has been a time of great darkness, the Maya have also seen it as a time to cross-fertilize the seeds of the Four Directions and races of the planet. This difficult task they have seen as the beginning of a new nation of multicolored beings. The seeds of the Four Directions have ever since been mixing together to create the first rainbow people.

Prior to the arrival of the Spanish, the Maya and many other Native American groups entrusted certain families with sacred information and the responsibility to keep it secret so that it could not be destroyed or abused. Guidance to take this action came from a council of elders that had been meeting for thousands of years before the Europeans came to Turtle Island. The council was made up of representatives from all of the Indian nations from Nicaragua north to the Arctic Circle. From dreams, visions, and prophecies, the elders of the council had become aware that the newcomers would try to change their religion, so they kept the most profound parts of their religion and science in their hearts and did not speak about them to anyone.

More than five hundred years ago, Hunbatz Men's family was entrusted with safekeeping part of this wisdom tradition. He is the contemporary holder of the lineage, although now, because it is time, he has begun to share the secrets. "The eyes of modern civilization see only a short span of time," he says. "To the European-American culture, five hundred years seems to be a lot of time. But five hundred years is nothing in the eyes of the Maya.

"It is written in time and in the memory of the Indian peoples that our sun will rise again, that we will be able to reestablish our culture: its arts, sciences, mathematics, and religion. Mayan knowledge will come forward again. It is for this reason that we of the Amerindian communities are once again uniting to reestablish our entire culture."

Chapter Three

Rainbow Heritage, Rainbow Destiny

Native American elders are not the only visionaries who have walked and worked on Turtle Island. The founders of the United States were also imbued with uncommonly high vision and spiritual sensitivity. They had respect for esoteric tradition as well as for the future. While the Constitution and the Declaration of Independence are evidence of their vision, some of the spiritual foundation they established has remained obscure.

The founders of the United States of America were steeped in the ancient spiritual traditions of the European continent. As widely reported, of the fifty-six signers of the Declaration of Independence, fifty-one belonged to the brotherhood of Freemasons, which was established in America under the guidance of Francis Bacon. Bacon saw the colonies as a testing ground for the spiritual principles of government that had been passed down from the ancient mystery schools in Greece, Egypt, and Chaldea. Many of the founders were also well versed in numerology, astrology, and other spiritual sciences—disciplines which have since been condemned as heresy by science, and seemingly vanished from public life (with the exception of former President Ronald Reagan, who routinely relied on astrological advice relayed to him by his wife, Nancy).

When the founders laid the cornerstone of the US Capitol building, their ceremony closely followed occult traditions and Masonic ritual. George Washington himself presided over the event while wearing a powdered wig and Masonic apron. According to researcher David Ovason in his book *The Secret Architecture of Our Nation's Capital*, as the city of Washington was built the major roadways were oriented to fixed stars. At least 23 important representations of the astrological zodiac and over 1,000 zodiacal and planetary symbols were incorporated into the Capitol and other key governmental buildings. Washington D.C. is a city of the stars—just as stars were placed on the flag, a constant visual reminder of something deeply held. The founders clearly intended to send the generations to come a metaphysical message of importance.

Likewise, the development of the U.S. Constitution was a conscious spiritual undertaking. In subtle but meaningful ways, the founders

FIGURE 2. *Wearing a Masonic apron, George Washington lays the cornerstone for the U.S. Capitol building. Fresco in the U.S. Capitol by Alan Cox, reprinted courtesy of the Architect of the Capitol.*

sought to join the high esoteric and exoteric traditions of Europe with some of the traditions of Turtle Island. While the European heritage offered order and intellectual rigor, the Turtle Island tradition offered democracy and tolerance for differences in race, spirituality, and point of view—virtues often lacking in the European dispensation of the 1700s.

The essential message of the rainbow is both implicit and explicit in the nation's spiritual history and destiny. Viewed in the context of the Legend of the Rainbow Warriors, the mission of the United States can be seen as to synthesize the cultural and spiritual heritage of the various races from around the globe, and to forge from this synthesis a new, stronger richer soul archetype. If such a synthesis is to go forward, it must rest upon a foundation of tolerance and mutual respect, spiritual qualities that develop not from theory but from experience.

Because the founders recognized the essential importance of tolerance, they began the Declaration of Independence with the statement: "We hold these truths to be self–evident: that all men are created equal…" Ultimately, so esteemed was tolerance that the founders put a guarantee of it into the Bill of Rights. Later in our history, as we moved into the twentieth century, we adopted the "melting pot" image as a popular national mythology. What has emerged from the melting pot, however, is hardly homogenous. It is, rather, a polyglot of differences, often in conflict, but with the potential to complement each other—a nascent rainbow culture.

An Angelic Presence

While he was encamped at Valley Forge, Pennsylvania with the Revolutionary Army in the winter of 1777, George Washington, first President of the United States, had a powerful, prophetic vision of an angelic presence. He reported in a letter to a friend that one cold night while he was alone, an archangel appeared and showed him a vision of three great crises of the republic: the American Revolution, the Civil War, and a third crisis, even greater than the previous two.

This story is documented in the December 1880 edition of the *National Tribune.* The article is based on the word of Anthony Sherman, who was at Valley Forge at the time of the reputed vision. Although some historians have expressed doubts about the authenticity of the experience, according to Sherman, Washington himself made careful record of the angelic encounter:

> I do not know whether it is owing to the anxiety of my mind or what, but this afternoon, as I was sitting at this table engaged in preparing a dispatch, something seemed to disturb me. Looking up, I beheld standing opposite me a singularly beautiful female. I would have risen but the riveted gaze of the being before me rendered volition impossible. I assayed once more to address her, but my tongue had become useless. Even thought in itself had become paralyzed. A new influence, mysterious, potent, irresistible, took possession of me. All I could do was to gaze steadily, vacantly at my unknown visitant. Gradually the surrounding atmosphere seemed as though becoming filled with sensations, and grew luminous. Everything about me seemed to rarify, the mysterious visitor herself becoming more airy and yet more distinct to my sight than before.
>
> Presently I heard a voice saying, "Son of the republic, look and learn," while at the same time my visitor extended her arm eastwardly…
>
> The scene instantly began to fade and dissolve, and I at last saw nothing but the rising, curling vapor I at first beheld. This also disappearing, I found myself once more gaping upon the mysterious visitor, who, in the same voice I had heard before, said, "Son of the republic, what you have seen is thus interpreted. Three great perils will come upon the republic. The most fearful is the third. The help against the third peril comes in the shape of Divine Assistance, passing which the whole world united shall not prevail against her. Let every child of the republic learn to live for his God, his land, and union." With these words the vision vanished, and I started from my seat and felt that I had seen a vision wherein had been shown to me the birth, progress and destiny of the United States.

The perils of the vision are generally understood to be the American Revolution, the Civil War, and a third yet to come. According to Sherman,

Washington's notes give no indications to suggest what the third peril might be or when it might occur.

Shared Traditions

George Washington, Thomas Jefferson, Benjamin Franklin, and other founders were inspired in their work not only by the European esoteric tradition but also specifically by the Confederacy of the Haudenausaunee. Known more popularly as the League of Iroquois Indians or the Iroquois Confederacy, the Haudenausenee inhabit the territory now known as New York state and southern Canada.

According to the oral tradition of the Haudenausaunee, long before the light-skinned race arrived on Turtle Island, the indigenous peoples of the Northeast had reached a crisis. Blood feuds between clans and a harsh, vindictive justice had made the society unsafe.

At this time, about three hundred years before the arrival of the Europeans, a male child was born to a woman of the Wyandot people living on the north shore of Lake Ontario. The child grew up to be a wise leader, so revered that his name is now spoken only in ceremony. He is generally referred to simply as the Peacemaker. With his companion, Hiawatha, the Peacemaker was able to "straighten the minds" of the most angry and fearsome of the people. He eventually brought all the people together under a set of principles known now as the Great Law. The Great Law embodies many noble ideas, including the following:

- The Giver of Life—the Creator—did not intend that people abuse one another. Therefore, human societies must form governments that prevent the abuse of human beings by other human beings and that ensure peace among nations and peoples.

- Peace is the product of a society that strives to establish reason and righteousness. "Righteousness" refers to the shared ideology of the people using their purest and most unselfish minds.

- All people have a right to the things they need to survive— even those who cannot or do not work. No people or person has a right to deprive others of these things: food, clothing, shelter, and protection.

- Human beings should use every effort to sit in council about, arbitrate, and negotiate their differences. Force should be resorted to only as a defense against the certain use of force.

- Chiefs or leaders are the servants of the people. Everyone has a right and a responsibility to participate in the workings of the government.

The Peacemaker's concepts of moral justice were penetrating, far-sighted, and ennobling of everyone in the community. In conjunction with the Great Law, The Peacemaker also put forward a system of government that was a complex formulation of participatory, rather than representative, government. Later in history, when the idea of the United Nations was proposed at the end of World War II, researchers were asked to find models in history for such an organization. The only working model they could find was the Haudenausenee Confederacy.

Likewise, earlier in history, when the founders of the United States set out to create a new form of democratic government, a form that the Europeans had not yet experienced, they looked to the wisdom of the Peacemaker and the example of the Iroquois Confederacy. Many of the spiritual and legal principles that guided the Confederacy then—and that still guide it to this day—served as inspiration for the Constitution of the United States.

Historian Gregory Schaff, Ph.D., author of *Wampum Belts and Peace Trees: George Morgan, Native Americans and Revolutionary Diplomacy*, conducted fourteen years of research on the authenticity of this aspect of US history. Schaff's work culminated in his 1990 testimony before the U.S. Senate Committee on Indian Affairs. As a result of his convincing evidence and testimony, Congress passed a resolution that was signed by President George Herbert Walker Bush. With the resolution, for the first time in history, the U.S. government officially recognized that many principal ideas for the U.S. Constitution came from the American Indian people.

The Great Seal
If symbols are the language of dreams, and if the founders of the United States can be said to have been motivated by an American dream, then

the Great Seal that appears on the back of every dollar bill is a symbolic expression of that dream. The Great Seal can provide keys to understanding the spiritual traditions the founders built upon, and the future they envisioned.

In 1782, Benjamin Franklin, Thomas Jefferson, and Charles Thompson were commissioned by the very first US Congress to design the official emblem of the new nation. Their commission became the Great Seal of the United States, the official impression that attests to the authenticity and legality of any agreement entered into by the United States government. The seal has been in continuous, legal use since it was established.

The Great Seal is a metal disc with vivid images on both front and back. For the front of the seal, Franklin, Jefferson, and Thompson selected the eagle. Long sacred to Native Americans, the eagle represents power and spiritual vision. It flies higher than all other birds and is the only creature that can look directly into the sun. The eagle on the seal grasps a banner in its mouth reading *E Pluribus Unum*, meaning "out of many, one."

The reverse of the seal bears the image of a four–sided pyramid, representing the material world. The all–seeing Eye of God at the capstone of the pyramid suggests the founders' intention that spiritually

FIGURE 3. *The Great Seal of the United States. The official emblem of the nation, designed by Benjamin Franklin, Thomas Jefferson, and Charles Thompson. Tradition holds that the seal offers a unified set of symbolic clues to the spiritual intention of the founders.*

informed vision serve as a guide to the affairs of the nation at all times. The location of the eye further suggests that spiritual vision be a guide for and be given priority over the abundant material life symbolized by the pyramid. This side of the Great Seal demonstrates that the founders saw America as a revolutionary undertaking. The motto they placed beneath the pyramid reads *Novus Ordo Seclorum,* "the new order of the ages."

In esoteric studies, thirteen is a number that signifies transformation. Thirteen is used thirteen times on the Great Seal of the United States: in the number of stars, arrows, olive leaves, berries, levels of the pyramid, letters in *E Pluribus Unum,* letters in *Annuit Coeptis* ("the Eye of Providence favors our undertaking)" and so forth. Was it a coincidence that the United States started with thirteen colonies?

Although it was designed long ago, the Great Seal was seldom seen until Henry Wallace, the secretary of agriculture under President Franklin D. Roosevelt, suggested during the 1930s that it be placed on the dollar bill. Wallace was a student of the ageless wisdom and appreciated the importance of the Great Seal's symbolism. Ever since the seal has been a visible part of the nation's daily commerce.

Corinne McLaughlin and Gordon Davidson are the founders of The Center for Visionary Leadership in Washington, DC, and the authors of *Spiritual Politics: Changing the World from the Inside Out.* Mclaughlin and Davidson have investigated the nation's early days extensively, pondered its hidden mysteries, and expounded upon them back in the 1980s in a scripted slide–tape show entitled *The Spiritual Heritage and Destiny of America.* As they put it, our national spiritual destiny is "to demonstrate to the world the unity of many races, religions and classes of people living together in cooperation and harmony, respecting the divine presence in all life."

McLaughlin and Davidson wrote that "we as Americans have gone deeply into materialism and are now learning the lessons of working creatively and lovingly with matter. America must transform materialism into unselfishness and commitment to the good of the whole." They believe that the separation of church and state in our founding documents was not meant to remove Spirit from government but rather to free the state from the control of dogmatic religion and to allow a more universal expression of Spirit.

Points on the Eagle's Compass

As we move beyond the millennium, few if any political leaders are articulating the kinds of high vision that animated the founders of the nation. Perhaps this is to be expected. According to the mythology of the rainbow, we are in a time of transition, just now entering a New Age, a new order of the ages. The rainbow legend avers that this age is not about great leaders but is rather a time when individuals and groups will be called upon to exercise intelligence, intuition, and free will in the service of humanity. Each must find his or her own way to serve family, neighborhood, nation, and planet. In the context of this legend, the national challenge contains two seemingly paradoxical elements for individual citizens: the urge to be free, unique individuals, and at the same time the impulse to find a path of service that benefits all the people.

While the United States may have powerful symbols like the soaring eagle and the Great Seal, the mythology of the rainbow suggests that we are not likely to have many national leaders who are capable of focusing our attention on the inner meaning of those symbols and the absolute importance of embodying the qualities they symbolize. The Rainbow Warriors legend suggests there is little point in waiting for a savior-leader like George Washington, Abraham Lincoln, or a Joan of Arc to come to our rescue. Such heroes are unlikely to arrive. We are all going to have to find our own ways through this transition to a new time, using the spiritual resources that lie within each of us.

What happens within the heart of the Earth or within a melting pot is frequently turbulent. When heat is intensified, alchemical processes take place. Strong currents begin to mingle. There can be violent collisions, explosions, and rapid shifts. In our era—not just in the US but throughout the world—the melting pot is at a rolling boil. Racial, religious, environmental, and economic elements are all mingling furiously in the pot.

As we pass through this crucible of history, if enough Americans accept and consciously seek to fulfill the founders' dream of alchemy and union, to reestablish the nation on a path toward its destiny, then in all likelihood the United States will remain a beacon, an inspiration to other peoples, and other nations. The beacon is an image much in keeping with two of most popular national symbols: Liberty, who lifts

FIGURE 4. *Messenger. The American Bald Eagle is a symbol of central importance for both ancient and modern America. Flying higher than any other of the winged ones, the eagle is the only creature of flesh and blood that can look directly into the sun. For Native America, the eagle represents a spiritual messenger who is said to bring the sacred pipe, a symbol joining the basic forces of the universe: the bowl of the pipe represents the feminine forces; the stem represents the masculine forces. Four colored streamers on the stem honor the four races of humanity living in harmony. In modern America the eagle retains high respect as a symbol for life, liberty, and the pursuit of happiness. Painting by Scott Guynup.*

her light by the eastern gate, and the eagle on the wing overhead. For thousands of years, soaring eagles showed the way onward and upward for the people of Turtle Island. Eagles still fly today, albeit over a ravaged earth.

Chapter Four

A Legend Aroused

In the early 1970s, under circumstances both curious and compelling, the Legend of the Rainbow Warriors crossed the amorphous line from myth to worldly substance. Through an environmental organization that came to be known as Greenpeace, the legend found a heartbeat first in Canada and the United States, then finally throughout the world.

The saga began in late 1969 when the U.S. government detonated a one-megaton nuclear bomb on a tiny island named Amchitka, off the west coast of Alaska. As it happened, this was—and still is—one of the most earthquake sensitive areas in the world. To many observers, it seemed patently stupid to explode massive nuclear bombs along the delicate fault line extending from Amchitka to the Alaskan mainland. As it happened, the nuclear blast in 1969 did not cause an earthquake, but it did raise a groundswell of protest in Canada and the US.

Then in 1971 the United States announced plans for another test blast on Amchitka, a blast code-named Cannikin that was to be five times stronger than the 1969 blast. Many people believed something had to be done to stop it. Among those who felt called to action were Canadians Jim and Marie Bohlen, Irving and Dorothy Stowe, and Paul Cote. They formed the "Don't Make a Wave Committee," a name intended to remind people that if the nuclear blast caused an earthquake, it would probably also bring a *tsunami*—a surging seismic tidal wave of titanic force.

Members of the committee began attending public hearings to protest the proposed five-megaton Cannikin blast and then they decided to take direct action. Specifically, they elected to secure a boat and sail directly to Amchitka to blockade the blast.

At one of the planning meetings held in Vancouver, British Columbia, the group searched for another name for the organization. As Jim Bohlen later explained, "the name 'Don't Make a Wave Committee' was a lot of words that didn't mean much. People didn't really relate to it, didn't know what it meant. So the group was trying to think of something that was more generic, that people could understand." Eventually, a young Canadian social worker named Bill Darnell came up with the name "Greenpeace." Because the name conveyed the group's broad goals succinctly, it stuck.

At 4 p.m. on September 15, 1971, after months of preparation and extensive media coverage, the ship *Phyllis Cormack*—now sporting the new Greenpeace logo—hoisted a green, triangular sail and slipped away from the dock in Vancouver. The first of hundreds of Greenpeace adventures had begun.

Just Before It Was Too Late

Among the small band of activists on board the *Phyllis Cormack* was Robert Hunter, a columnist for the *Vancouver Sun* newspaper. Since the first nuclear blast at Amchitka, he had written many an impassioned article about the environment and the state of the world.

On October 2, 1969, he had authored a column with a sharp assessment of what lay ahead: "Politicians, take note. There is a power out there in suburbia, so far harnessed only to charity drives, campaigns and PTAs, which, if ever properly brought to bear on the great problems of the day, will have an impact so great the result of its being detonated (like the Amchitka A-bomb test) cannot be predicted."

Back in that pivotal year of 1969, Hunter had a farm in western Canada. One day a vagabond dulcimer maker came through and presented him with a slim volume entitled *Warriors of the Rainbow*, by William Willoya and Vinson Brown. The itinerant craftsman told him the little book would change his life, and then he left, never to be seen again.

Hunter took the book with him when he boarded that first Greenpeace expedition. The book contained several accounts of an ancient prophecy that seemed uncannily relevant to the ship's crew. The book told the story of how a Cree grandmother named Eyes of Fire had predicted that there would come a time when the Earth would be ravaged of its resources, the sea blackened, the streams poisoned, and the deer made to drop in their tracks—all due to greed-driven technology. Eyes of Fire had seen that at the time of these happenings, the Indian people would have all but lost their spirit. But, just before it was too late, they would find their spirit again and would begin to teach others how to have reverence for Mother Earth. Under the symbol of the rainbow, all the races of the world would band together to spread these great teachings. These teachers would be the Warriors of the Rainbow, and they would ultimately, after a great struggle, bring an end to the desecration of the Earth.

Robert Hunter was struck by the connection between this Indian legend, the reality of the world condition, and the work that he found himself and Greenpeace doing. He passed his copy of the book around the ship so others could read it. The next day, rainbows appeared several times as the boat chugged through a maze of inlets and channels. Hunter later wrote, "It all did seem somehow magical." There they were, journeying over the ocean waters on a campaign, just as the legend prophesied, to help save Mother Earth.

Did Hunter and the crew members believe the Cree legend: that one day the Indians would find their lost spirit and teach the light-skinned people how to have reverence for Mother Earth, and that people would go forth as Warriors of the Rainbow to protect the natural world? According to *The Greenpeace Story* by Michael Brown and John May, on some days Hunter believed the legend and on other days he did not. In the beginning, he found being part of Greenpeace difficult and discouraging. There were many obstacles and tremendous resistance to what they were trying to do. In the early 1970s environmentalists were widely considered to be the lunatic fringe.

"The Cree legend says nothing about how difficult the passage to the new time will be," Hunter has explained. "It does not tell what the

PHOTO 7. *Greenpeace Initiation into the Kwakiutal Tribe. At the end of the first Greenpeace expedition in 1971, the members of the crew were invited to the Longhouse of the Kwakiutal Indian people to be initiated as honorary members of the tribe. Photo by Robert Keziere/Greenpeace.*

voyage from a world bent on destroying itself to a world committed to saving itself will be like. It just says it will happen." In later years, Robert Hunter became Greenpeace's liaison with the Native American community. From time to time, during the years 1973 through 1977, he served as chairman for Greenpeace.

That first voyage of the *Phyllis Cormack,* by all accounts, was tremendously challenging. The ship was plagued by mechanical failures, the crew became weary, and they were arrested by the U.S. Coast Guard for failing to notify Customs of their arrival in U.S. waters. The weather turned bad. Then, frustratingly, the U.S. government postponed the atomic blast several times. Morale waned. Many crew members had to get back to their jobs. Finally, reluctantly, on October 12, 1972, the Greenpeace crew voted to return to Vancouver.

On the way back to port in Vancouver the crew was invited to dock at Kodiak Island, where a banquet sponsored by the city honored their bravery. Later, in a stunning moment of mythic coincidence, at Alert Bay they were greeted by the Kwakiutal Indians, who anointed them at a sacred ceremony in their longhouse and made them honorary tribal members.

Though the isolated crew had become discouraged and had developed a sense of defeat, their voyage had been front-page news in Canada. They had generated tremendous goodwill not only in the north, but also in the United States and elsewhere around the world. In fact, public support had been so strong that, back in British Columbia, Irving Stowe had been able to raise the money for another, faster, Greenpeace ship. Thus, just as the *Phyllis Cormack* returned home, the *Edgewater Fortune* set off with another crew for a second try at blocking the explosion at Amchitka. On November 6, 1971, while the *Edgewater Fortune* was still seven hundred miles away, the five-megaton nuclear bomb was detonated. The fledgling Greenpeace organization had been unable to stop the blast, but it did succeed in its larger goal. The protests had grown so strong that the U.S. government decided to stop its nuclear tests at Amchitka.

The Rainbow Goes to Sea

At the beginning of 1978, a growing Greenpeace, by now an international organization, purchased a twenty-year-old Scottish trawler named the *Sir William Hardy.* The 160-foot ship was moved to a new dock, refitted for environmental work, and painted white and dark green. A bright rainbow was emblazoned on her side and a dove carrying an olive branch was painted across her bow. She was then re-christened the *Rainbow Warrior.*

On May 15, 1978 Greenpeace's new ship sailed under the Tower Bridge of London on her maiden voyage. Shortly thereafter, in the first of many exploits, she intercepted the *Gem,* a British-owned nuclear-waste ship. The *Gem* was on its way to foul the international waters of the ocean with two thousand tons of radioactive waste—waste that would remain radioactive for millennia. That same year the *Rainbow Warrior* successfully opposed the Norwegian hunt of Grey seals on the Orkney Islands and set off on campaigns to help save the harp seals, the whales, and the dolphins. It also initiated efforts against oil, chemical, and nuclear pollution.

Greenpeace has become famous—and in some corporate head-quarters infamous—for its daring exploits and dramatic stunts, all intended to call attention to the systematic, industrial destruction of the Earth and the creatures who share life upon it. In accordance with the group's central philosophy, all of the confrontations have been non-violent. The following list is a small sample from the thousands of actions Greenpeace has undertaken all over the world:

- They parachuted into the construction site of the largest nuclear power plant in the world, the Darlington Generating Station in Ontario, Canada.

- They marched to and then occupied the Trident nuclear submarine base in Washington State.

- They released three hundred dolphins trapped in nets off the Japanese coast before fishermen returned to massacre them.

- They climbed the scaffolding surrounding the Statue of Liberty in New York harbor while the statue was being restored, and hung a huge banner from it, proclaiming "Give me Liberty from Nuclear Weapons. Stop Testing."

- They plugged the waste discharge pipes of the Monsanto chemical plant in Boston, Massachusetts, to prevent the daily fouling of Boston Harbor.

- They scaled industrial smokestacks across Europe to hang banners that spelled out "STOP"—a demand for an end to the steady onslaught of bitter emissions that causes the rains to turn dark and acid.

As of the year 2000, Greenpeace had three million supporters in 158 countries around the world, with about 1,000 full-time staff linked by an international computer network. The organization is actively involved in some thirty international conventions for the protection of the environment.

Greenpeace is an independent campaigning organization that uses non-violent, creative confrontation to expose global environmental problems, and works to bring about important changes in consciousness and politics internationally. Greenpeace campaigns arise out of global imperatives to protect our oceans' ecosystems, to stop global warming, to save ancient forests, and to end nuclear threats and toxic pollution.

Greenpeace has also taken a leading stand in the crucial debate over genetically engineered foods. Will we have the right to exercise free will and choose the foods we eat? Or will those foods remain unlabeled and thus unidentifiable by the public. As of the year 2001, close to 70% of the processed foods in our supermarkets contain genetically engineered components. No one can possibly know what the consequences of this will be in seven generations. Meanwhile corporations continue to patent plants, animals, cells, and DNA sequences—so that they may own and profit from them. Greenpeace has taken strong and generally skillful stands to inform public debate on these key issues.

Over the years, Greenpeace has consistently worked in the face of danger. While boldly confrontational, the group has remained nonviolent. It has sought to radically transform our understanding of the world and the direction in which it is heading. As the group's official history states, the Greenpeace message is simple and powerful, an echo of the Great Law of the Haudenosenee people: "Everyone has the right to clean water, fresh air, and a safe future."

PHOTO 8. *The Rainbow Warrior. Agents of the French government planted bombs aboard the Rainbow Warrior on July 10, 1985. The bomb explosions sank the ship and killed Greenpeace photographer Fernando Pereira. Photo © 1985 Miller/Greenpeace.*

Rainbow's End?

In July of 1985, the *Rainbow Warrior* arrived at Auckland Harbor in New Zealand on its campaign for a nuclear-free Pacific. The ship's crew was planning to gather support from well-wishers in New Zealand and then to join a peace fleet that would sail to the Moruroa Atoll, where France had been exploding nuclear bombs steadily since 1966. Greenpeace was making this protest for the fifth time in thirteen years, and apparently the French had run out of patience with the organization's interference.

The ship received a rousing welcome when it arrived at the harbor. But then four days later, at about 11:45 PM on July 10, 1985, an explosion ripped a six-by-eight foot hole in the hull of the *Rainbow Warrior* while it lay at anchor at Marsden Wharf in Auckland Harbor.

After the explosion, Greenpeace photographer Fernando Pereira ran to the door of the engine room to survey the scene. He turned swiftly and started back to his cabin, apparently to rescue his cameras. It was a fatal turn. Moments later, a second explosion rocked the

Rainbow Warrior, and the boat sank, incredibly fast. Thirteen people on board scrambled ashore quickly and safely, but hours later, divers from the New Zealand Navy found Pereira's body. The cause of his death was listed as drowning.

Despite the organization's record of dramatic, risky and confrontational tactics, Pereira became the first member of Greenpeace ever to be killed while working on a campaign. At the time of the bombing, New Zealand's prime minister, David Lange quickly labeled the incident "a major criminal act with terrorist overtones." In response to the sinking, Greenpeace International chairman David McTaggart offered two blunt sentences: "We campaign against violence. We will not be stopped by it."

Two days after the sinking, a couple, both officers in the French military, was arrested and charged with murder and arson in connection with the bombing. As the investigation proceeded, it was revealed that the plot to sink the *Rainbow Warrior* extended to the highest levels of French government. The scandal implicated not only French agents Dominique Prieur and Alain Mafart, but also Admiral Pierre Lacoste, head of the French secret service and the French Minister of Defense, Charles Hernu. French President Francois Mitterand himself was nearly forced to resign.

You Can't Sink a Rainbow

Eventually, the original *Rainbow Warrior* was towed out to sea and sunk eighty feet beneath the waters of New Zealand's Matauri Bay. The boat forms an artificial reef there, a sanctuary for marine life.

On July 10, 1989, four years to the day after the bombing, Greenpeace launched a new ship, also named the *Rainbow Warrior*, in Hamburg Harbor, West Germany. At the launching ceremonies, Rebecca Johnson, head of Greenpeace's campaign against nuclear testing, said "The name *Rainbow Warrior* symbolizes that you cannot sink an idea, or remove it by force."

The new boat was a 181-foot Scottish trawler built in 1957. It cost $4 million to purchase and refit the ship. To reduce energy demand, Greenpeace had the boat redesigned to carry three masts and specially designed sails. The arrangement yields fuel savings of as much as 80 percent. Greenpeace paid for the new flagship with some of the $8.2 million in damages it received from the French government.

Like its predecessor, the new *Rainbow Warrior* is based in the Pacific, where it sails to combat nuclear and chemical pollution and to thwart drift-net fishing by Japan, Korea and Taiwan.

When the first *Rainbow Warrior* sank in Auckland Harbor, it took with it any illusions that the global healing process would be an easy task. As the smoke cleared from the explosions, it became starkly apparent that the struggle would be, in essence, a war for the fate of the Earth. Could that war be fought and won with peaceful means—with confrontational but nonviolent means? Many thousands of Rainbow Warriors aver that it is possible.

PHOTO 9. The new Rainbow Warrior. The new Greenpeace ship sails the seas to call attention to the nuclear and chemical dumping that has fouled waters around the world, and to demonstrate new ways. Photo by Culley/Greenpeace © 1989.

Mythology may have been a helpful source of inspiration for Greenpeace in the beginning, but the organization was founded in response to real world problems, and it has remained focused on those problems. Greenpeace has, appropriately, maintained a low-key emphasis on the legend, directing its collective resources to halting the reality of the poisons that glut our world, at the same time promoting technologies that are in harmony with the Earth—technologies that will make life clean, possible and pleasant for future generations.

Chapter Five

A Calendar Calls

Through the daring actions of Greenpeace and other environmental organizations, millions of people awakened to the perilous condition of the Earth's environment and were spurred to direct, creative action. Yet toxins continued to glut the soil, the air, and the water; most people slumbered through the 1970s and 1980s as if the problems of the Earth belonged to others. Then mid-way through 1987 something happened that woke up many more millions—something that served as sort of a cosmic alarm clock for legions of rainbow warriors.

The terms New Age and Age of Aquarius are well known, if not particularly well understood, but few people have heard of the Age of Flowers. Yet, if there is substance to one of the central legends of the land now known as America, the Age of Flowers began to unfold in 1987 with an event that some Native American wisdom keepers say was of crucial importance.

According to various students of Turtle Island's mystical heritage, the Age of Flowers began in August of 1987 with a sharp acceleration of the energy at work in the world. This acceleration is said to have initiated a period of wholesale change that would shake the world for 25 years, until the winter solstice of 2012, as the old gives way to the new.

Arising from the ancient cultures of Central America, the prophecies concerning the transition from one age to another are recorded symbolically in the Mayan and Aztec calendars—works of high mathematical sophistication. Because of their logical elegance, their direct relation to precisely measurable celestial cycles, and the depth of the information they contain, these calendars—in conjunction with the pyramids of the Americas—are considered by metaphysical scholars to be principal repositories of the esoteric teachings of the Western hemisphere. In this

FIGURE 5. *Keeper of Sacred Time. The great circular Aztec calendar has been recognized by mathematicians as being more precise, accurate, and sophisticated than the Gregorian calendar used by modern Western civilization. Along with the seventeen calendars of the Maya, who are the sacred keepers of time, the Aztec calendar pointed to a major shift beginning in 1987 and culminating December 21, 2012. Reprinted from* American Indian Design & Decoration *by LeRoy H. Appleton, courtesy of Dover Publications, Inc.*

light the southlands of Turtle Island, home to 20,000 or more magnificent pyramids and temples, can be seen as the Egypt of the Americas.
To be rightly understood the native teachings from the southlands
require a historical context, one provided by a facet of North America's
heritage given scant attention in textbooks.

Lord of the Dawn

More than a thousand years ago in the land now known as Mexico, the
Toltec tribe was led by a great king and prophet named Quetzalcoatl.
His symbol was a serpent covered with green feathers, representing the
union of Earth and Spirit. Around his head, like an aura, was a half-circle
crown of rainbow-hued feathers, sparkling with the full spectrum of
color. Called the Lord of the Dawn, Quetzalcoatl was thought to be a
Divine Son who was carrying out the will of Creator.

This king was described as a white man, with a beard, who wore
long robes, and taught of one supreme God. He also gave the Toltecs
many material gifts, such as their calendar, and instructed them in all
manner of arts, sciences, and social customs. Members of the Mormon
Church, and many other people, believe that Quetzalcoatl was actually
Christ visiting the Americas during what are known as his lost years,
from age 12 through 30. In the *Book of Mormon* and other publications
they assert this claim in some detail. As with the legends that have been
passed down about Jesus Christ, a central part of the myth of
Quetzalcoatl is his promise, at death, to return at a time when the
world is in great need.

In Central America the figure of Quetzalcoatl is known as Kukulcan
or Gucumatz. South America was also visited by a teacher of similar
description who goes by a variety of names: Sume in Brazil, Bochia in
Columbia, and Con-tici (Kon–tiki), or Viracocha in Peru. In North
America this teacher is sometimes referred to simply as "the Pale One."

Though the myths of the Americas are in some ways indistinct,
many students of this continent would agree that Quetzalcoatl represents the Americas' most spectacular culture hero. His legend is certainly
the one with the most widespread influence. In the regions we know
today as Mexico, he taught a religion of love, and formed two holy
orders: the Jaguar Knights and the Eagle Knights. Like the famed
Knights of the Round Table—and at about the same period in history—

these Central American knights were dedicated to the search for spiritual strength and to performing deeds of honor, mercy, and kindness. Along with all who believed in Quetzalcoatl's teachings, they became members of the Fellowship of the Tree of Life, symbolized by a real tree in Oaxaca, Mexico. This tree, *El Tule,* is said to embody the love and unity of people who merge their hearts together and work to fulfill the teachings of the Creator.

As history has amply recorded, this emphasis on the heart was in time distorted by the Aztecs in a ritual of bloody sacrifice. William Irwin Thompson expressed that distortion vividly in his book *Blue Jade*

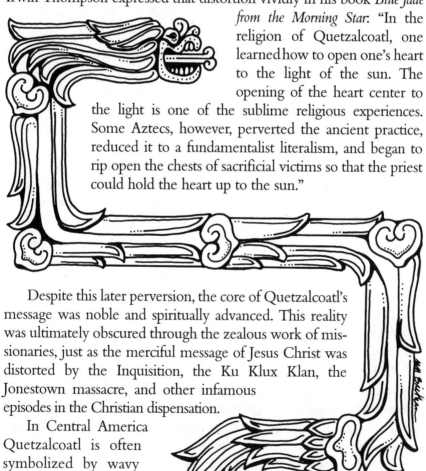

from the Morning Star: "In the religion of Quetzalcoatl, one learned how to open one's heart to the light of the sun. The opening of the heart center to the light is one of the sublime religious experiences. Some Aztecs, however, perverted the ancient practice, reduced it to a fundamentalist literalism, and began to rip open the chests of sacrificial victims so that the priest could hold the heart up to the sun."

Despite this later perversion, the core of Quetzalcoatl's message was noble and spiritually advanced. This reality was ultimately obscured through the zealous work of missionaries, just as the merciful message of Jesus Christ was distorted by the Inquisition, the Ku Klux Klan, the Jonestown massacre, and other infamous episodes in the Christian dispensation.

In Central America Quetzalcoatl is often symbolized by wavy lines, much like the glyph for the astrological

FIGURE 6.
Quetzalcoatl. The rainbow feathered serpent.

sign of Aquarius. The lines represent the energy of natural electricity—the pure energy of creative intelligence. This is also the meaning of the Feathered Serpent image. The serpent represents the Earth because it lives so close to the Earth, and uses its whole being to go forward in life. The feathers, which are the feathers of an eagle, represent Spirit because the eagle, of all creatures, flies closest to the heavens. In the symbol of the Feathered Serpent, Earth and Spirit are therefore brought together, integrated in a good way, much as they are in the symbol of the rainbow. The rainbow suggests that all the colors and pathways of creation are to be respected and honored. Quetzalcoatl is said to be the embodiment of the serpent rainbow beam of cosmic intelligence—the bio–electric sperm of the universe fertilizing the womb of the Earth.

Interestingly, the symbol of the Feathered Serpent is strongly akin to the central healing symbol of Western medicine: known as the caduceus or staff of Hermes, it is the universal and familiar emblem of the modern physician.

In his book, *The Way of the Physician*, Dr. Jacob Needleman poses two provocative questions: Why is this symbol used, and where does it come from? "The staff of Hermes," he answers, "was one of the principal symbols of the work of self-perfection. The two serpents represent the two fundamental forces of universal nature—one moving outward, away from the Source, and the second moving back toward union with the Source.

FIGURE 7. *The Caduceus, or Hermes' Staff, the universal symbol of the medical profession.*

"The world of nature was understood [in the time of the classical Greek civilization] as the stage where these two opposing forces constantly war with each other. Out of this warfare the whole of the created world arises through the mediation and reconciliation of a third movement symbolized by the figure of a dove resting atop the staff in between the heads of the serpents." In many later representations of this symbol, Dr. Needleman points out, the dove is replaced by a pair of wings. In Christian terminology, this winged principle of reconciliation is known as the Holy Spirit, or Holy Ghost.

The classical Greek symbol actually derives from the much more ancient wisdom of the Vedic tradition of India. In that tradition, the spiraling snakes represent the lunar and solar forces at work in the energy body of all human beings. The serpent force, seen as residing in the body's central channel or spinal cord, is the power of kundalini as it spirals up the body until the force reaches the crown of the head, from which the spirit takes flight and is expressed in the world.

Taken as a whole, the image of the physician's caduceus is strikingly similar to the symbol of the Feathered Serpent. According to the prophecies of Turtle Island, now is the time when this correspondence is becoming plain.

When the World Seemed to be Dying

Quetzalcoatl is said to have foretold many of the important events to occur in the thousand years following his death. In particular, he prophesied that he would return one day in the same manner that he left: over the eastern ocean. Before he returned, he said, bearded white men would come in boats with sails like great white wings. They would conquer the Indians and force on them a different religion—a beautiful religion, but one that many white men would not live up to themselves.

Later, Quetzalcoatl prophesied, when the world seemed to be dying from abuses of the science brought by the light-skinned conquerors, the Tree of Life (*El Tule*) would wither and die, symbolizing the end of one age and the start of another. As understood by the Toltecs, our present world has been preceded by four other worlds or creations, all of which have been destroyed as they became spiritually corrupt—the last time by a great flood which covered the Earth.

Quetzalcoatl further prophesied that after his passing the world would go through thirteen fifty-two-year cycles of increasing light and choice, followed by nine fifty-two-year cycles of increasing darkness and trouble: the Nine *Bolontikus* (Hells). According to some students of the calendars that record this prophecy, the last of the Nine Hells came to an end on August 16, 1987. At that point, they say, we entered a twenty-five year epoch of transition to the next phase of world evolution: the era, or world, of the Sixth Sun.

As Quetzalcoatl foresaw it, our fate during the time of transition, would be, as ever, in our own hands. We could destroy the world through selfish thoughts and actions or we could come into harmony with Divine order and all the creations of the Earth. We possess free will and thus could choose one or the other.

Crisis in Consciousness

In an unpublished manuscript entitled *Ancient Mexican Prophecy for the New Age*, researcher and writer Eugene Johnson links the Central American prophecies to the persistent legend of Atlantis. According to many versions of the myth, the continent of Atlantis was located in the middle of what we know today as the Atlantic Ocean.

Johnson believes Atlantis was the home port of Noah and other boat people who survived the great flood. This flood is remembered in many cultures—African, Australian, Native American, and Chinese, as well as Greek, Jewish, and Christian—as the event that destroyed the world before this one, the world of the Fourth Sun, in Aztec terminology. When Atlantis went under the ocean waves, some of the people who were wise and good were said to have escaped in boats and eventually to have seeded the future civilizations of Europe, Egypt, Australia, the Orient, and the Americas. Johnson believes that indigenous American cultures had a prophetic sense that their new world (Fifth Sun) would one day also come to an end. Their prophecies, he says, are encoded in the architecture of their Central American pyramids and in the mathematical symbols on their calendars.

Johnson writes that the city of Teotihuacan, northeast of Mexico City, served for centuries as a primary seat of learning and religious ceremony for the Americas. At its zenith around AD 600, it was probably the largest city in the world. The name Teotihuacan means "birthplace of the gods." According to legend, the city and its elegant pyramids were built at the beginning of the Aztec Fifth Sun, after the Atlantean cataclysm brought the era of the Fourth Sun to an end. They were intended to commemorate the start of that particular new age (Fifth World) and to set forth in their proportions and design a prophecy of the spiritual plan for the generations to come.

Teotihuacan is said to be a power center, connected by ley lines (energy pathways) to hundreds of other holy sites around the world such as Stonehenge, Chaco Canyon, Niagara Falls, Machu Picchu, Mount Khatadin, Mount Shasta, and the Egyptian pyramids. Johnson says Teotihuacan, with its mysterious ceremonial pyramids, served as a primary focal point for the subtle energies that infused the Earth during the summer of 1987.

No one knows for sure what the new world cycle will bring, according to Johnson. But in his manuscript he did indulge in some cautious speculation: "It's unreasonable to expect that suddenly, in 1987, the diseased conditions which plague the world will evaporate, leaving us in a blissful state of perfection. The world must go through a 'cleansing' of some sort to open up sufficient space for new development to begin."

The event of August 16, 1987, which came to be known as Harmonic Convergence, was said to have begun a twenty-five year cycle when subtle energy currents would be released, accelerated, and intensified to work in the world. The keynote for this prophetic period, Johnson suggested, would be a crisis in consciousness, a period of intense spiritual action in the world and in the souls of the people.

In technical terms, using a related Mayan calendar, August 16, 1987 was the last day of the nineteenth *Katun* of the thirteenth *Baktun*. The dawn of August 17, 1987 was the beginning of the last part of an entire 5,125–year cycle depicted in one of seventeen Mayan calendars. In other words, according to this particular Native American system, August 16, 1987, marked the end of a cycle of Earth's history that began in 3113 BC, and it initiated a brief transitional phase leading to the year 2012. By the Aztec system of reckoning, we are in transition to the era of the Sixth Sun; by the Hopi system of reckoning, we are entering the era of the Fifth Sun.

Harmonic Convergence

In his popular book *The Mayan Factor: Path Beyond Technology,* poet and visionary José Argüelles, Ph.D., set out an elaborate interpretation of the events prophesied in Native American calendars. Argüelles wrote that since the beginning of what he calls the Mayan Great Cycle, the Earth and its inhabitants have been passing slowly through a beam of cosmic energy 5,125 years wide. The cosmic intention of that beam of energy, he wrote, has been to accelerate the vibratory rate of subtle energies on Earth and to bring them into harmony with the vast spiral of the Milky Way galaxy, of which our sun is part.

PHOTO 10. *José and Lloydine Argüelles.*
Photo by Chris Hatfield.

In the summer of 1987, Argüelles posited, we would begin a radical quickening of energy and consciousness that would last twenty-five years until December 21, 2011. This was his interpretation of the final date in one of the prophetic Mayan Calendars, though other sources give the end date as 2012, 2013, and 2026. At any rate, according to Argüelles, at that time our galactic synchronization will be complete. Whatever parts of our civilization have survived the era of transition will be in harmony with the great spiral of the galaxy, a spiral evident in the winds, in the waters, and in all living forms on the Earth—even in the spiral of DNA in human cells. These are the natural energy patterns represented in the spiraling snakes of the caduceus. Argüelles believes that by the end of the Native American calendar we will have found a path that allows us to go beyond the limits and perils of the machine age—a path that blends Spirit with technology, heaven with Earth.

One critical moment in this transition, Argüelles wrote, occurred at sunrise on the morning of Sunday, August 16, 1987. That moment began what he called Harmonic Convergence, the accelerated release of potent cosmic energies. With his wife Lloydine, José Argüelles helped organize multimedia arts festivals around the world to celebrate this event and to create focal points for the arrival of the cosmic impulse. His original press release for Harmonic Convergence went out at the same time a massive supernova (exploding star) was being discovered in the sign of Aquarius, the sign of the New Age. In the press release he wrote of Harmonic Convergence enigmatically as "the point at which the counter–spin of history finally comes to a momentary halt, and the still imperceptible spin of post-history commences."

According to Argüelles, from the moment of that August sunrise, the world began to undergo intensified transformative chaos, the climax of the disastrously corrupt materialism of the industrial world. This global chaos, he wrote in 1987, would include the collapse and regrouping of major governments, as well as deindustrialization and demilitarization. But, he added, "it is precisely at the climax of matter, the fateful moment of materialism's full ripeness, that the highest and culminating purpose of the entire historical cycle will reveal itself." This new revelation, or paradigm, Argüelles said, will be a unified planetary consciousness, marked by an inspired and illumined humanity.

Ceremonial Time
Consider the context of the mythology and prophecies associated with Harmonic Convergence. Overlooked for many years, these prophecies came to the fore at a time when issues of Central American policy occupied a critical place in public consciousness—a time when Mexico and all of Central America were in great economic and social unrest. In combination with other world events, the scene appeared set for something dramatic to happen.

The years just before Harmonic Convergence were marked with some stunning events that deeply penetrated the collective unconscious. In the summer of 1985, for example, six Soviet Cosmonauts shared an amazing encounter while they orbited the Earth in the *Salyut 7* space station. As reported widely in the Soviet press and in *Parade Magazine* in the U.S., the Cosmonauts all observed a band of angels. "What we saw," reported a spokesperson for the six scientists, "were seven figures in the form of humans, but with wings and mist–like halos, as in the classic depiction of angels. Their faces were round with cherubic smiles." Twelve days later into their mission, they saw the angels a second time. Discounting skeptics' allegations that they experienced a mass hallucination, Cosmonaut Svetlana Savitskaya reported, "The angels were smiling, as though they shared in a glorious secret."

Likewise, in April of 1986, just a year before Harmonic Convergence, a tragedy of staggering proportions unfolded at the Chernobyl nuclear reactor in the Soviet Union. A fire and the subsequent release of nuclear radiation seized global attention. In the world's most serious nuclear accident, Reactor 4 released about 50 tons of radioactive dust and debris, which was carried by winds and rain to virtually every country in the Northern Hemisphere. While commenting on the incident in

The New York Times, reporter Serge Schmemann told of his meeting with a prominent Russian writer, who had produced a tattered old *Bible* and with a practiced hand turned to the Apocalypse. The writer encouraged the reporter to listen carefully to what he promised would be an incredible passage: "And the third angel sounded, and there fell a great star from heaven, burning as if it were a lamp, and it fell upon the third part of the rivers, and upon the fountains of waters; and the name of the star is called Wormwood; and many men died of the waters because they were made bitter." In a dictionary, the writer turned to the Ukrainian word for wormwood, a bitter wild herb used as a tonic in rural Russia. The reporter bent over and saw the word written plain: Chernobyl.

No doubt about it. By the time 1987 arrived, late in the millennium, the world was awash in anguish, greed, uncertainty, and faint hope. Powerful energies were at work in the world. Whether they were taking cues from the nightly news, the Bible, the Sphinx, or outer space, most people already felt that they were living in a time of momentous transition. But transition to what? No one will know for sure, of course, until we get wherever we're going. But at the time of Harmonic Convergence many people on many spiritual paths—Rainbow Warriors—had already dedicated their lives to helping steer Planet Earth toward a higher destiny, a spiritual destiny. Therefore, thousands of people used the prophesied shift to a New Age—whether the shift was a genuine cosmic event or just a working hypothesis—to engage in spiritual action consecrated to healing.

Turning Point

Shortly after the prophetic year of 1987 began, astronomers observed a rare and riveting phenomenon in the skies over the Southern Hemisphere: a supernova, the explosive death of a star. According to scientists, in that spectacular explosion, a distant star released in a few seconds as much energy as our sun puts out in ten billion years. Supernova 1987a—in the sign of Aquarius—was the signal celestial event of a wild year, which peaked in a summer notable for stunning news

The summer of 1987 was the season when the five billionth baby was born on Planet Earth; the summer used syringes and dead dolphins began washing up on shore; the summer world debt grew to dizzying

PHOTO 11. *Supernova 1987a. A rare celestial event, the explosion of a distant star, marked the early part of the year of Harmonic Convergence. Astronomers said Supernova 1987a, visible to the naked eye only in the Southern Hemisphere, exploded 175,000 years ago; it took the light that long to reach Earth. Mythologists pondered the possible meanings of this omen. Photo by Marcelo Bass/National Optical Astronomy Observatories.*

heights; the summer AIDS and miniskirts were juxtaposed; the summer the ozone hole grew larger, the forests smaller, and the 36 wars more intense; the summer we learned that one-third of the Earth's water was polluted; the summer that scolding preachers became mired in petty sexual and financial failings; the summer Americans began shooting at each other on the freeways.

In the summer of 1987, most people had a sense that we had reached a fateful turning point in our collective destiny. Pollster George Gallup, Jr., summed the situation up in July when he told a Minnesota prayer breakfast that, based on his polls, he found most Americans felt we were facing "a moral and ethical crisis of the first dimension."

The summer of 1987 also brought word from ancient mystical sources that deliverance was at hand—that the dawning of the New Age was only a matter of weeks away. This news hit home with a sizable segment of the nation and world. The prophecies were a laser beam of hope in a messy and murky world. After all, a lot of people had been waiting impatiently for something called the New Age since the 1960s. There was already a vast reservoir of pent–up expectation. In the context of the world's history, and amidst the jagged rhythm of the summer's news, was it at all surprising that there was such a rush to respond?

Harmonic Convergence had tremendous romantic appeal. It promised to empower people acting out of love and strength to bring peace and harmony into the world. Most of the people who participated were not only sincere but also mature and skilled—in the arts and crafts, the sciences, the mysteries, in all walks of life. The Flower Children and all their relations had done a lot of growing and learning since the Summer of Love in the late 1960s. Harmonic Convergence was a great excuse to express their deepest aspirations, to reconnect the Woodstock Nation, and to take action with the skills they had acquired.

José Argüelles put it this way: "The world had been without vision for so long that Harmonic Convergence awakened in many different kinds of people a stirring in the breast, an ache in the heart, a recollection of ancient power and legendary meaning that had long been past."

As the summer built to a crescendo, thousands began to fervently believe that with purification and prayer they could make a difference in the fate of the world—that they could tip the scales in favor of an age of peace.

National Fruit Loops Day

With a queer and unbecoming bitterness, Gary Trudeau, who had come of age in the Sixties, had the characters in his comic strip "Doonesbury" label August 16 as the "Moronic Convergence—a sort of National Fruit Loops Day."

Following his lead, much of the mass media fairly choked on hyperbole, cynicism, and inaccuracy as they reported on the buildup to the event. The criticisms had an oddly perverse twist, as if the critics believed there was nothing to believe in at all. As the summer of 1987 wore on, Harmonic Convergence took on a life of its own, far bigger than any one prophecy, timetable, or spokesperson. Word raced from meditation group to newsletter to network. At Digital Equipment Corporation, for example, there were hundreds of reported entries about the event on the in-house computer system in a time before the internet had come into its own. The word was out.

Was Harmonic Convergence just a wild-eyed New Age fantasy? Was it real but too subtle to perceive? Was everyone chasing after a false

Christ? Or had the New Age begun to blossom at last? There are a thousand answers to these questions, none of them certain. But one thing is for sure: the date served as an effective focus for prayer around the world. Thousands upon thousands of people decided they didn't care whether anything cosmic was happening or not: they were going to make their prayers and then teach and support a way of life that would be at peace with the Earth and all the creations who share it. They were going to take action as Rainbow Warriors.

The Great Prayer

While meteor showers creased the mid-August night, people sat and waited—alone, by the hundreds, by the thousands. They waited across North America, Central America, South America—across the entire planet. That such a massive and far-flung gathering could have happened seemed improbable if not impossible at the start of summer 1987. But such was the combined power of the grapevine and the mass media that by mid-August many millions knew about Harmonic Convergence and had a chance to participate. Ultimately, so bombastic was the ballyhoo that many people were waiting for UFOs to sweep down from the heavens, for Extraterrestrials to dramatically materialize, and for celestial pyrotechnics on the order of Armageddon. Others were expecting more subtle but no less potent forces to somehow work their way into the world.

Wherever the people were, when dawn came they beat on drums, they rang bells, they meditated on flowers, and they raised their voices in thanksgiving and prayer. They were the Harmonic Convergers, the Rainbow Warriors, and they made a mighty prayer to start the blossoms unfolding in an Age of Flowers. They believed that ripples from their great prayer would start to spiral through an extensive network of people dedicated to healing the Earth.

Plenty to Spare

The participants in Harmonic Convergence were trying to reach a critical mass, to get the fabled "hundredth monkey" in line at a sacred time and in a sacred place. The legends said it would take 144,000 people to reach this critical mass. Did enough people turn out?

According to Wendy Call, who worked at the Harmonic Convergence coordination office in Boulder, Colorado in 1987, "Yes, with

A Sampler of Harmonic Convergence Gatherings

Global Gatherings	*Number of Participants*
Great Pyramid, Egypt	1,500
Delphi, Greece	350
Reykavik, Iceland	800
Eiffel Tower, Paris	400
Machu Picchu, Peru	100
Teotihuacan, Mexico	10,000
El Tule Tree, Oaxaca, Mexico	125
Ayer's Rock (Uluru), Australia	2,000
Mt. Warning (Wollombin), Australia	600
Sydney, Australia	3,000

Gatherings in the United States	
Niagara Falls, New York	300
Colorado Springs, Colorado	500
Shelburne, Vermont	250
Enchanted Rock, Texas	350
Redlands, California	100
McCall, Idaho	300
Serpent Mound, Ohio	600
Stone Mountain, Georgia	100
Chaco Canyon, New Mexico	3,000
Mount Shasta, California	5,000
Fallsburg, New York	3,000
Mount Monadnock, New Hampshire	300
Cadillac Mountain, Maine	800
Mount Wachusett, Massachusetts	200
Mystery Hill, Salem, NH	300
Bangor, Maine	400
Haleakala Volcano, Hawaii	5,000
Santa Barbara, California (outside President Ronald Reagan's Western White House)	144

FIGURE 8. A sampler of Harmonic Convergence gatherings. Thousands of other groups and individuals gathered to contribute to the overall energy field of consciousness and ceremony created at Harmonic Convergence, August 16, 1987.

plenty to spare." She began her work in March, so she saw the event transform from a quiet plan for an art event to a mass-media global celebration. She said there were gatherings all over America and at sacred sites all over the world. "There were hundreds and hundreds and hundreds of ceremonies," she said. "We have no way of verifying it, but we are certain that there were well over 144,000 people out there. From the calls and letters I saw, my general sense is that people had a wonderful time. It was a very good and positive experience. Many people report that they were surprised by the broad range of people involved—old, young, fat, thin, hippie, business, family, children—people from all walks of life."

Based on hundreds of individual reports, the experience of Harmonic Convergence appears to have been as diverse as the human community itself. Some greeted the sun with solemn meditation, others with drums and chanting or with crystals laid out in grids. Yet others greeted dawn at a Sun Dance, or with rock music and New Wave sunglasses as they watched the sky and the Earth. Some few responded as if the event were a chance to lecture, or as if they were at a rock concert or a special performance of the human circus. Most felt they were sharing sacred moments in sacred places. And then, inevitably, morning gave way to afternoon.

Chapter Six

On the Threshold

With a wild flurry of media attention and feverishly inflated expectations, Harmonic Convergence unfolded on mountaintops and at sacred sites around the world. Then it dropped from view, as if it had been a fantasy weekend and nothing more—as if that's all there had been to it.

Yet many people who greeted the dawn with prayers for peace and songs for the Earth, and who considered both the ancient prophecies and the modern portents, say they saw something more. They say Harmonic Convergence was not a one-day event but rather the start of an intense, all–encompassing 25-year epoch of evolution. They say that if we can move with the energy that was released, if we can bring it into our lives in a balanced manner—and likewise honor the Sacred Hoop of creation—then the transition to a new time will be less traumatic, more harmonious.

Are they right? Did a specific cycle of world history come to an end? Did the summer of 1987 mark a sharp acceleration in the rate of world change? Was there a great mystical influx of energy? Has a discrete era of transition begun? Are we truly on the cusp of a new age? In the years since Harmonic Convergence there have been many dramatic world events. But can those events be correlated in any meaningful way with Harmonic Convergence?

Even among metaphysical scholars, questions remain over whether Harmonic Convergence was a real event and whether José Argüelles and others correctly interpreted the ancient calendars of Turtle Island. About this controversy, Argüelles once responded, "As far as the dates on the calendar, it doesn't really matter whether I was right or wrong. Something happened and something's happening. Just look around."

Just Looking Around

Many people reported seeing things at sunrise on August 16, 1987: rainbows, dragonflies, clouds shaped like dragons. All of these are considered to be symbols of Quetzalcoatl, the Lord of the Dawn, the legendary Central American leader whose spirit is said to be tied to fulfillment of the calendar. As suggested in advance by many observers, thousands of people did in fact have profound visions and dreams during Harmonic

PHOTO *12. Harmonic Convergence at Niagara Falls. As people marked Harmonic Convergence at Niagara Falls, they were greeted by a rainbow, a familiar phenomenon at the falls. Photo © 1987 by Robert Ford.*

Convergence. Some people also say they saw UFOs, specifically at Mount Shasta in California and at Teotihuacan in Mexico.

The year that followed Harmonic Convergence was marked by disruptions that consistently hinted of Apocalypse. Arabs and Israelis clashed on the ancient prophetic Temple Mount in Jerusalem. Sikhs and Hindus warred upon each other in the sacred Golden Temple of Amritsar in India. A group of machine-gun toting fanatics attacked pilgrims in Mecca, setting off a bloody massacre at the time of the Haj, the sacred pilgrimage of the Moslem religion. In Tibet, normally pacific Buddhist monks came to believe that all of their ancient prophecies had been fulfilled; in frustration they rioted violently, attempting to throw off Chinese domination and restore the Dalai Lama to authority.

In the aftermath of the summer of 1987 the tone and undertone of world news has frequently conveyed the sense that we are living in ominously momentous times. On May 23, 1988, for example, CBS News reported that America's bird population was in dramatic decline and that we had cause again to fear a Silent Spring. "The birds," intoned Dan Rather, "are sending us a warning." The same might be said about the whales and dolphins washing up on the shores of our fouled oceans, about the weakened forests, and about our poisoned lakes, streams, rivers and wells. The damage is vast.

Halfway through the twenty-five year epoch of transition, at the start of the 21st Century, by conservative estimate, over 27 million people live in bondage around the world—more slaves than at any other time in history. U.S. industry continues to release, every single year, about 24 billion pounds of toxic substances that are strongly suspected of causing developmental and neurological problems. The oceans of the world have begun to experience explosions of toxic algae blooms that have had catastrophic impact on fisheries; meanwhile, beds of sea grass are rapidly shrinking in many coastal areas around the world, eliminating a vital nursery for the marine species that are the foundation of the food chain. Powerful thunder and lighting storms are regularly appearing in the High Arctic region—something never before witnessed by science or the traditional Inuit people who inhabit this region. Many scientists caution that all these are clear warning signs of massive ecological breakdown.

As the immune system of Planet Earth has been attacked and weakened, so, too, is our human immune system attacked and weakened by the effluent of industrial culture. As of the year 2000 the number of people suffering from allergies or asthma—as a result of compromised immune systems—has reached pandemic levels.

Meanwhile, storms bearing winds of 140 MPH and more have slammed England, France, Japan, Bangladesh, and the Philippines; unusually high winds have also ripped through Australia and the heartland of America. Earthquakes and other natural disasters have continued to rattle the planet with regularity. Volcanoes have flared to life. The protective layer of ozone around the Earth has dissolved at an astonishing and unarguable pace, vastly increasing the flow of ultraviolet fire to the Earth, and raising the incidence of skin cancers and also weakening the plants that support human and animal life. Amphibian populations continued to decline, and especially in the case of frogs and toads, to mutate grotesquely; dozens of primate species also face collapse, according to Conservation International, a scientific group based in Washington, DC.

Evidence supporting the likelihood of the Greenhouse Effect has mounted. A US Congressional report released in the summer of 2000 said that global warming in the 21st century will cause drastic changes in the climate of the US, including severe droughts, floods, mass migrations of species, substantial shifts in agriculture, and widespread erosion of coastal zones. What were just dark dreams in the summer of 1987 are now the realities that fill newspaper columns at the axis of the millennium. Responsible scientific forecasts have been off in only one respect: the effects of global warming are hitting faster and harder. Meanwhile, over this stretch of time general environmental deterioration has continued around the globe at a queasily swift pace.

So sorry was the state of the world that late in the 20th Century the Kogi came forward. The Kogi are an indigenous people who live on Sierra Nevada de Santa Marta in Columbia, the highest seaside mountain in the world, which is set dramatically on the shore of the Caribbean sea. Having retreated to the remotest parts of their mountain 400 years ago, the Kogi are said to be the only native civilization in South America not demolished by the Europeans who settled the continent.

As the Kogi understand their lives, it is their duty to look after the mountain, which they call 'The Heart of the World.' They speak of themselves as "Elder Brother" and refer to the new–comers as "Younger Brother." They have survived by keeping themselves isolated. But shortly after Harmonic Convergence, in the early 1990s, they realized that it was time to send a message to the Younger Brothers. They could see that something was wrong with their mountain, with the heart of the world. The snows had stopped falling and the rivers were not so full. If their mountain was ill, they observed, then the whole world was in trouble.

The Kogi invited a reporter for the British Broadcasting Company (BBC), Alan Ereira, to visit them and to produce a widely broadcast video program entitled *The Message from the Heart of the World: The Elder Brothers' Warning*, and also a book, called *The Heart of the World.*

After allowing the reporter to record images of the sophisticated culture that they have maintained for centuries, the Kogi elders spoke their message to the BBC cameras. In 1991 that message was widely shown on the BBC, and in America on the Public Broadcasting System (PBS).

The Kogi elders said, "We look after nature, and we see that you are killing it by what you do. We are asking you to stop. We can no longer repair the world. You must.

"We are here to give a warning to all the younger brothers and to all the world. You are taking out the Mother's heart and cutting her up when you dig for the gold and all the minerals. Remember the Mother; she is the mind inside all of nature and also fertility and growth. We see the Earth is dying and losing her strength because of this. The water down below is drying up. When she dies, you will die. We don't know when the world will end, but it will end soon if you go on this way."

"Younger brother is violating the basic foundation of the world's law…We tell you, we the people of this place, Kogi, Asario, Arhuaco: that is a violation…Younger brother thinks, 'Yes! Here I am! I know much about the universe!' But this knowing is learning to destroy the world, to destroy everything, all humanity.

"The earth feels, they take out petrol, it feels pain there. So the earth sends out sickness. There will be many medicines, drugs, but in the end the drugs will not be of any use. The Mamas say that this tale must be learned by the Younger Brother."

Transformational Themes
In the years following Harmonic Convergence, the onslaught of global change has been staggering. Political and economic upheaval has visited the Soviet Union, China, Africa, Iraq, Central America, Europe, and the Middle East. Banks, insurance companies, and corporations all have been rocked to their foundations by the forces at work in the world, and forced to restructure. Change has not, however, been limited to human institutions. Consider the following snippets from the realm of science:

- In 1988 anthropologists discovered human fossils in the Qafez Cave in Israel that they dated using a technique called thermoluminescence (heat and light). Previously, most scientists had thought humanity (Homo Sapiens) was no more than forty thousand years old. The fossils proved that we've been here at least one hundred thousand years. In 1991 scientists discovered other fossils at Lake Baringo in Kenya that extended by 500,000 years the age of the genus Homo, the genus that lead to and includes modern humans. Previously, the earliest known Homo fossil was dated at 1.9 million years old. The newly discovered fossils pushed the date back to about 2.5 million years. These findings forced anthropologists to recast their theories of evolution.

- The most widely accepted theories about the age of the Earth set it at about 4.5 to 4.6 billion years. But in the spring of 1988, Japanese scientists discovered ten diamonds (crystals) in Zaire, Africa, that are at least six billion years old.

- For decades, scientists contended that North America had only been inhabited by human beings for the past twelve thousand years—since the last Ice Age subsided. But in the spring of 1991, archeologists digging in a cave at Orogrande, New Mexico, found convincing evidence—fire circles and spear points—that humans have lived on this continent for at least the last thirty-five thousand years. This discovery is prompting a complete revision of American prehistory and buttressing the statements of Native American elders, who have long claimed that their ancestors have lived on this land for tens of thousands of years.

• The Torus project heated gasses to a record temperature of two hundred million degrees Fahrenheit, which is almost ten times hotter than the temperature of the sun. Scientists from fourteen European nations cooperated in the experiment, which was designed to replicate the complex process that takes place in the sun's core. This process, it is hoped, can someday be used to generate electricity.

• Physicists at the NEC Institute in Princeton, NJ, broke the generally accepted speed limit of the universe: the speed of light. In July, 2000 they sent a pulse of laser light through cesium vapor so quickly that it left the chamber before it had even finished entering it. The researchers said it was the most convincing evidence yet that the speed of light—supposedly an ironclad rule of nature—can be pushed beyond known boundaries. The results of the experiment were published in the journal *Nature.*

• Columbia University began a systematic search of the Milky Way by activating the Very Large Array radio telescope. They hoped to piece together a comprehensive picture of our home galaxy and thereby place the sun rightly in the context of the four hundred billion other stars that make up the giant spiral of the Milky Way.

• Japanese researchers discovered evidence that the heart of our Milky Way Galaxy is in fact a huge black hole that spews a magnetic tornado of energy seventy-five million-billion miles long. This spiraling maelstrom of magnetic energy, the researchers said, bends and waves like a hose on a plane perpendicular to the relatively flat spiral of our galaxy.

Photo 13. M81. *A typical spiral galaxy of about 400 million stars in the constellation Ursa Major (the Great Bear, or Big Dipper). The galaxy is said to be similar to the Milky Way, the home galaxy of our sun and planet Earth. As astronomer Carl Sagan once memorably put it, there are "billions and billions of galaxies in our universe." Photo by National Optical Astronomy Observatories.*

• The National Geographic Society changed the official map of the Earth. The map in use for most of the last century wildly distorted the proportions of countries far from the equator, causing the Soviet Union to appear twice as large as it is in reality and the oceans to appear much smaller than they really are. Cartographers said the new map would give human beings a far more realistic view of their planet.

To these developments could be added major breakthroughs in superconductivity, nuclear fusion, the demolition of a cherished myth with the discovery of two identical snowflakes, and certainly the large-scale efforts to unravel the genetic code of plants, animals, and humans.

In June, 2000 a team of scientists said that they had produced the first full–length record of all 3.2 billion chemical units in human DNA. As the feat was announced President William Clinton commented, "today we are learning the language in which God created life." Investors on Wall Street immediately drove up the price of stocks for these companies, hoping to maximize profits from the research.

Mayan Daykeeper Hunbatz Men, who has a tradition–rooted view on this era of transition, cautions against going too fast with exploitation of the human genome. "It took nature millions of years to develop the genes in a good way. Now scientists motivated by money think they can change it all in two years. That's not a good motivation when you are dealing with something sacred." Hunbatz says that ancient Maya teachings address the hazards of manipulating the stuff of life. He believes, in fact, that the word "gene" may ultimately derive from the Mayan *ge ne*, which denotes the sacred spiral of life that is evident not only in the double helix of our genes, but also in the form of the Milky Way galaxy, of which our Sun is part.

Hunbatz cautions all who are involved in biotechnology, and the public which will bear the consequences of this work: "Don't play with sacred knowledge unless you have understanding, humility, and the permission of Spirit as it is manifest in the life forms you wish to change. Otherwise, playing God will come to no good. You cannot anticipate all the effects when you make genetic alterations."

Mythology of the Transition

In the mythology of Harmonic Convergence, one of the central themes is the expansion of human consciousness. José Argüelles postulated that over the twenty-five years of transition, human consciousness would have the opportunity to expand from the relatively narrow confines of our solar system to the more universal perspective of the galaxy. Many of the developments since the summer of 1987 have indeed tended to erode the narrow confines of traditional beliefs. For example:

   • A group of Protestant and Catholic scholars concluded that Jesus was not, in fact, the author of the Lord's Prayer, as the gospels proclaim. This prayer, the foundational petition of Christians to God the Father, was instead ascribed to an earlier Hebrew teacher identified only as "Q." Likewise, the scholars agreed that the predominant narrative strand running through Genesis, Exodus, and Numbers is a composite of earlier literary sources. These composite chapters were assembled by a writer they identify as "J." In all likelihood, this first author of the *Bible* was a woman.

- In America and elsewhere around the world, people began a fundamental reassessment of recent history beginning with the arrival of Columbus in the New World. For the first time, evidence became widely available that Columbus's reign over Hispaniola (the island of modern-day Haiti and the Dominican Republic) had been an unmitigated horror. In the years immediately following 1492, his harsh policies and practices led directly to the extermination of the native population from Hispaniola (an estimated 125,000 to 500,000 human beings). The actions of Columbus set a pattern that was continued in large measure by the explorers and settlers who followed him.

- Ireland's fiery Protestant minister Ian Paisley shocked the world community when he disrupted the address of Pope John Paul II to the European Parliament in 1988. The Pope had barely begun his speech when Reverend Paisley rose with a red poster in hand, and loudly denounced "the holy father" as "the Antichrist."

- The Vatican ordered Dominican priest Matthew Fox to remain silent for one year, and then eventually excommunicated him. His heresy was teaching that "women and men must give birth to a creation-centered religious vision," as opposed to a vision based on fears of hell. Reverend Fox had preached that the Church's unbending emphasis on human sin, including the concept of original sin as opposed to the concept of an original blessing (life itself), had blinded it to travesties such as genocide and the rape of the Earth.

- The 1980s and 1990s were characterized by a sharp increase in UFO sightings, including dozens by reliable authorities from the military, the law, and science, and the government of France. One knowledgeable observer commented that the credible evidence had mounted so high that UFO news should be on Page 1 of the newspapers, not back with the comics.

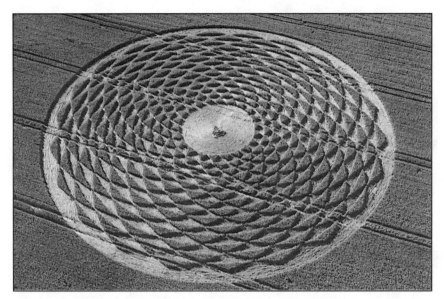

PHOTO 14. *A typical crop circle in a wheat field, photo taken in July, 2000 at Woodborough Hill, Wilts, UK. Photo © 2000 by Steve Alexander*

- Mysterious crop circles began to appear with increasing frequency in the grain fields of England and in many other nations, including the United States and Canada. In 1991 two artists claimed responsibility for the circles. Their assertion that they had created all of the circles as a hoax failed to convince careful observers. How, skeptics wondered, could two men with hand tools have created as many as seven hundred huge, meticulously laid out geometrical patterns, on several continents, without leaving footprints and without breaking a stalk of grain? Every summer since, elegant, elaborate crop circles have continued to appear by the hundreds, around the world year after year. Despite the occasional hoax and efforts to discount their significance, crop circles continue to be inadequately explained. Consequently, at the turn of the millennium, crop circles remain an exquisite mystery.

This list of astonishments could be expanded to include yet other developments that are dramatically changing public perception of the way things are. Altogether the changes imply a pattern in keeping with the theme of Harmonic Convergence: radical change in our world and in our relationship to the universe.

Campaign for the Earth

All this and much more has come to pass since Harmonic Convergence. Was Harmonic Convergence, therefore, a real cosmic event? Are we consequently in the midst of a complete global transformation? At this early stage of the millennium, when claims and counterclaims beset the public from every side, it seems ill-advised to grasp too quickly for pat explanations. So often they are illusions. Yet the tone, pattern and force of world events calls out for careful consideration. What is going on here?

In his book *The Mayan Factor: Path Beyond Technology,* José Argüelles wrote that, based on his study of the Amerindian cultures, he believed that after August 16, 1987, the currents of world events would combine to create a cresting wave of world history. He said there would be a shift in energy frequency at Harmonic Convergence, and that after that the institutions and structures that were not in harmony with the circles and spirals of the emerging world would be shaken. The storm of transformation, he predicted, would intensify.

Argüelles suggested that the time we are living in should be thought of not so much as a time of destruction, but rather as an opportunity to change the world by bringing forward alternative ways of life that are in harmony with nature. He urged people to take the energy of the epoch and use it creatively, not just for themselves, but for the community of life. This, he said, is the mandate of the rainbow warriors.

There Is Truth in This

In many Native American cosmologies, there is an understanding that civilizations have risen, and then fallen, on Earth before. These civilizations have been destroyed primarily because they developed technology and then employed it without wisdom. Many traditional elders say we are obviously again in a period when technology dominates life and is generally being applied without wisdom.

Doñ Alejandro Cirilo Perez is president of a Maya Elders Council in Guatemala, the sponsor of many Guatemalan orphanages, and a

PHOTO 15. *Doñ Alejandro Cirilo Perez. Author photo.*

widely respected Daykeeper, charged with keeping the prophecies and dreams of his people, as well as keeping time according to the intricate mathematics of the Mayan calendars.

A warm man who is noted for generosity of spirit, doñ Alejandro says the event called Harmonic Convergence did indeed mark an important turning point according to the tradition of the Mayan calendars. "There is truth in the prophecies about the rainbow and the rainbow people," doñ Alejandro says. "People from all of the Americas will unite with people from all the other nations, and they will realize that we are all family, brothers and sisters. This is not my personal vision, but a cosmic vision presented by all the elders—a vision that we all share.

"Big changes are coming in this frame of time. That's why it's important to talk now and tell people to respect Mother Earth, and to stop destroying the water, air, and mountains. We must respect all the creations of the Creator, and stop making those kinds of technologies that affect the solar rays that come to us on Earth. True scientists must think of our children. Care for each other. Love each other without dicrimination. That is my main message.

"We are in times of big changes for the Earth, big earthquakes and hurricanes, also big conflicts in politics and war. They [politicians] promise changes. But we know that at their big meetings, done in the name of making things better, they do not make changes that work. It's the same old thing. The people must make the changes themselves."

You Can See It, But You Have to Look

Although many native teachers believe we are moving into a new epoch of history, their understandings of this transition are varied. Some say we are moving from the Fourth World to the Fifth World, and others say we are going from the Fifth World to the Sixth World. Ultimately, these distinctions may be of small consequence. What emerges as important and universal is the theme of pervading change and the opportunities that result from that understanding.

One articulate spokesperson for this time of transition is Yehwehnode, also called Two Wolves or She Whose Voice Rides on the Wind. More widely, she is known as Grandmother Twylah Nitsch of the Seneca Nation, founder of the Wolf Clan Teaching Lodge. She believes we are moving from the Fourth World to the Fifth World, and she has much to share on this theme.

PHOTO 16. Grandmother Twylah Nitsch. Photo by Steven Schoff © 1987.

Grandmother Twylah first heard her family's prophecies of the Earth cleansing when she was just ten years old. If people lost their spiritual values, the prophecies warned, the Earth would be cleansed. The prophecies made a deep impression on her. "There have been a series of worlds," she explains. "The first time the sun cleansed the Earth, next the moon did, then water. The fourth time, this time, the Earth will be cleansed by all of these forces. Those prophecies also foretold that a band of people would come to this continent from the East. They wouldn't know who they were or what their future held. They would seek answers by digging into the Earth, the water, and the Moon—lacking any understanding about these powers. When they began digging into the fire secrets of the sun (nuclear fission and fusion), the prophecies say, it would create the next cleansing.

"Most people only know about the Third World, Atlantis, which was cleansed by the great flood. But altogether there are seven worlds in the history of the Earth. From the First World," Twylah explains, "we inherited the gift of beauty. From the Second World, we inherited family structure; thus, learning about the balance between physical and spiritual energy. From the Third World, we inherited clarity of purpose through self-discipline. In the Fourth World, we developed diversity of wisdom. The Fourth World, though, also spawned the syndrome of separation and control, creating wars and religions. We have now entered the time of the Fifth World, which began at Harmonic Convergence.

"North America and South America were the site of the First World. While we are now over the threshold of the Fifth World, there are obviously many hangovers still around from the Fourth World. In the Fourth World, the greatest division came when humankind became impatient and created a God—'Him'—out there somewhere, separate from men and women. We are not separate. But this had to happen in the history of the Earth. There were lessons that we needed to learn through this experience.

"There's a certain blindness now. People have their eyes closed. It's a disease. People say, 'Well, the world's a mess, but as long as it's not depriving me of food and shelter, I really don't need to do anything about it.' Yet we do need to make deep personal decisions about this. Some people choose not to see, to be blind, not to be responsible.

"In the Fifth World that is dawning illumination will be the central theme. Spiritual awareness will be common. Illumination radiates from the center. The focus is on truth—all the information in the world is useless without truth. We humans have to be willing to take a chance. What is wisdom? It's an inner knowing of truth, without a shadow of a doubt. But it can't stand alone; it's tied to the other qualities on the Medicine Wheel. This life is not a game but is based on the wisdom of the trees, the grasses, the stones, and all of life. Wisdom is also having a dream. If you have no dream, you can't tap into wisdom. If a person has an idea that flashes into their mind, that's the beginning of a dream. But they must bring life into the idea and develop the dream or it will pass on."

"Any time there is a drastic change," Grandmother Twylah asserts, "it takes the environment and the people within the environment about twenty-five years to have this transition occur—to have the trend really felt and appreciated by the people. So if trees are burned down, for example, and then new ones are seeded, it's going to take about twenty-five years, if they're untouched, before some of them will look like trees again. So it will take some time before we see the full influence of the illumination of the Fifth World. It's happening, and you can see it, but you have to look."

Chapter Seven

Message
of the Hopi

While he was alive, Hopi Grandfather David Monongye taught a simple lesson, not just to his adopted granddaughter Oh Shinnah, but to all who would listen. He told people, "We are all brothers and sisters. We are all flowers in Great Spirit's garden, and we share a common root. We have different gifts and colors, but we all share a root in the Earth Mother." Grandfather David was one of many in a long line of respected traditional Hopi elders.

Living on isolated and arid mesas in the part of Turtle Island now known as Arizona, the Hopi have a religion that is at once both simple and elaborate. Although TV antennas and other signs of the modern world are now in evidence in the villages, some few Hopi, whose name means "peaceful people," are still guided by understandings, or prophecies, handed down orally for long generations, much like the Kogi people of South America. Following what they believe are the original instructions of the Creator, they have lived plainly and respectfully for thousands of years in the desert. Many people believe that, although they are few in number, the traditional Hopi play a key role in the destiny of the world as messengers of peace.

To understand how this might be, one must first appreciate the way their elders understand history. Hopi elders believe that after a great flood purified the world before this one, the Creator appointed them guardians of certain sacred land—land that no one else wanted. At that time, they say, the Creator gave them some specific spiritual insights, along with some stone tablets bearing symbols depicting the way the future was likely to unfold.

Though there are disagreements concerning the exact interpretation of the symbols on the tablets, traditional Hopi elders agree that for hundreds of years world events have been unfolding as described by the symbols on the stones. In our times—as prophesied in the tablet's symbols—the world appears to be in a phase known as *koyaanisquatsi*, chaos. This phase of chaos leads to the Great Purification that marks the end of the present-day Fourth World. Perhaps this Great Purification may give birth to the world of the Fifth Sun. That's up to us.

As with the myths of Australian Aborigines and other tribal cultures around the world, Hopi tradition holds that in ancient days the rainbow of humanity was whole. All the people—red, white, black, and yellow—at one time recognized each other as brothers and sisters, and all spoke the same language. Eventually, events forced the people to part ways, but they all pledged that when they were reunited they would clasp hands again in a sacred handshake. Then all the brothers and sisters would work in harmony to bring together the material and spiritual aspects of the world by sharing what they had learned on their separate sojourns. The people would correct each others' faults and eventually live together again, side by side in fulfillment. Hopi elders say their oral tradition even specified the time and place where the reunion might occur.

Several years after arriving in Mexico in 1519, Spanish explorer Hernan Cortés directed Francisco Coronado to ride North in search of the legendary seven cities of gold, the "Seven Cities of Cibola." In 1540—just when the Hopi expected them—a patrol from the Coronado expedition headed by lieutenant Pedro de Tovar, and including seventeen horsemen and a Franciscan Friar, encountered the Hopi on a mesa not far from the village of Oraibi. The leader of the Hopi Bear Clan, who had gone out to meet the long-lost brothers, held out his hand in the sign of greeting specified by Hopi tradition (sometimes called the nakwa´ch). Rather than clasping the elders' hand in brotherhood, de Tovar apparently thought that the Indian was seeking a gift. He ordered one of his men to drop some trinkets into the elder's outstretched hand. With this botched exchange, many Hopi immediately began to perceive that their light–skinned relations had forgotten the ancient pledge. Some accounts of this first meeting even say that the Conquistadors soon became angry and drove the Hopi back up onto the mesas by charging them with lances.

FIGURE 9. Kokopelli, the Hopi flute–playing spirit.

Whatever actually happened, from the Hopi perspective the ramifications of this lapse of core memory by the white explorers were not long in coming. Based on their prophecies, the Hopi believed that if things began to unfold in this troubling way, there would come a day when they would be forced to develop the land under the dictates of a new ruler. For thousands of years they had held their land in a communal and religious way, sharing all resources and making ceremonies to help hold the Earth in balance.

Their prophecies of a change in their relationship to the land proved accurate when settlers began to stake claims across the southwest and then, in the late nineteenth century, U.S. Senator Henry L. Dawes of Massachusetts successfully argued in Washington that the Red Nations would never progress as they were, He said communal sharing of the land and other resources—the Indian way—involved no self-interest, and no profit incentive. In his view—and in the view of many in that day— the Indian people needed to cultivate material interests. One of Dawes intellectual compatriots, Merrill Gates, wrote of Native Americans: "We need to awaken in him wants. In his dull savagery he must be touched by the wings of the divine angel of discontent."

They hatched a plan to bring this about, and got to work. Thus, in 1890 the U.S. Congress passed the Dawes Act, which allotted a defined portion of land to each individual on a reservation. Private ownership of land became an enforced reality; sharing and common use were thus rendered outside the law. Greed, jealousy, and separatism soon invaded Hopi lands, and the lands of every other Native American tribe impacted by the law. A system that had worked and supported its peoples for generation upon generation came to an end; and the new system cast many Hopi into a spiritual and material poverty the likes of which they could never have previously imagined.

Signs They Watched For

The few remaining traditional Hopi elders believe that the world is perilously out of balance now, and that humanity is being tested again—just as we were tested by water and flooding in the world before this one.

According to Hopi understandings, the human race has passed through several stages of life since its origin. At the end of each stage, or world, life has been purified by certain acts of Great Spirit as a consequence of moral corruption, lack of respect for the balance of nature, and widespread greed turning people away from the instructions of Great Spirit to live simply, humbly, and reverently.

One Hopi teaching holds that the first world was destroyed by the sinking of the land, the second world by ice, the third world by flood. Stories about destruction of the world before this one by water are widely acknowledged as universal. Researchers have found over 200 versions of the flood legend around the world, including the Biblical account of Noah and the Ark, Plato's account of Atlantis, and enduring legends in Australia, China, India, South America, Africa, and among many Native American tribes. Although understandings and interpretations vary, some say the present-day fourth world (*Tewaquachi*) is to be purified by fire and ash (perhaps nuclear war), and others say by all four elements—earth, air, fire, and water—nature's own changes in response to human destruction.

To appreciate the relevance of the Hopi teachings one must see them in the general context of Native American history and lore. Contemporary Native American elders represent a direct link to what may be the oldest spiritual tradition extant, one that has been maintained on Turtle Island (North America) for thousands of years Most of the world's professed spiritual traditions are fairly recent. Islam is about 1,500 years old; Christianity is 2,000 years old; and Judaism is perhaps 2,000 years older. But the indigenous peoples of America lay claim to an unbroken tradition that goes back thousands of years before that. As recalled in the lore of many Native American tribes, in the beginning different groups of people were given responsibility for different parts of the planet we all shared. The Yellow people were given responsibility for the air, the Black people the water, and the White people the fire—an element now wildly out of balance as evidenced by the Greenhouse Effect, by dangerous UV radiation from the Sun streaming through the widening holes in the Earth's protective ozone layer, the burgeoning piles of hot nuclear waste, and innumerable other fiery manifestations. The Red people were given specific spiritual responsibility as keepers of the Earth. The Hopi live in the Four Corners region of Arizona, an area that, among Native Americans, is widely considered to be of central spiritual significance for all of the Earth.

Since the end of World War II when they were first publicly proclaimed, Hopi legends and prophecies have gradually assumed worldwide prominence. Many Hopi say that one specific sign they were instructed to watch for, a "gourd of ashes," was in fact represented by the nuclear bombs "poured out" upon Nagasaki and Hiroshima causing "everything to boil and be destroyed over a wide area"—the element of fire unleashed in war.

The Hopi were given specific instructions by way of their oral tradition. They were told that, when the modern world came to this time of great imbalance—*koyaanisquatsi*—they were to make four attempts to address the leaders of the world who would meet in a "great House of Mica (glass)" that would one day stand on the Eastern shore of Turtle Island (North America). That House of Mica, traditional Hopi believe, is the United Nations headquarters, housed in a New York City building with a distinctive glass façade (like the transparent mineral mica).

If the Hopi were recognized and permitted to speak, then according to their oral tradition they would be free finally to deliver a warning and a message that could help the people of the world rediscover and realign themselves with the original instructions of the Creator. The term "original instructions" refers not to any written or otherwise fixed code, but rather to the broad understanding that human beings exist in a universe of living spirit, that all things are sacred and related. Respect and harmony must prevail.

If the Hopi were not heard at the House of Mica, then according to the prophecies, "many shall be destroyed, after which real peace, brotherhood and justice shall be brought about." On the other hand, as with most prophecies, these consequences are apparently not absolute.

Some elders believe that the purification process at the end of this World can be averted, or at least lessened in severity, if people purify themselves individually of their own free will, and return to a sacred manner of living in good relationship with all things.

After the atomic bombings of Hiroshima and Nagasaki, Hopi spiritual leaders from various villages and religious societies met in December, 1948 for the first time in history. They met to compare their previously secret knowledge as per ancient instructions handed down through the generations. Thomas Banyacya was one of four men commissioned at that meeting to bring to the outside world the Message of Peace and the warnings for humanity revealed at this meeting. Banyacya had already taken courageous stands for peace in his life. As a youth he had been inspired by the great Hopi elder named Yukiuma—who had lived at the start of the 20th Century, and who some regard as "The Hopi Gandhi."

A native of the Hopi village of Moencopi, Banyacya attended the Sherman Indian School in Riverside, Calif., and then the all-Indian Bacone College in Oklahoma, where he was a star long-distance runner. At college he was disturbed by the lack of attention to indigenous cultures and helped establish a lodge where students could sing and perform traditional ceremonies.

In the 1940s, at a time when many Hopis were beginning to embrace modern ways even unto accepting the governmental jurisdiction of the United States, Banyacya remained steadfast in his devotion to the sovereignty of the Hopi. He spent seven years in prison rather than register for the draft in World War II. As he often explained, the Hopi, whose very name means "peaceful," reject fighting in wars, especially for another nation. His moral stand apparently had an impact. After writing a letter to President Dwight Eisenhower in 1953, Banyacya helped win an understanding with local

PHOTO 17. *Hopi Messenger Thomas Banyacya.*
Photo © 1994 by Lynn Wozniak.

Selective Service officials that any Hopi who requested classification as a conscientious objector would receive it.

For the rest of his life Banyaca held to his commitments, despite hardships and criticisms. He traveled widely to carry the Hopi message and in the process helped inspire a revival of traditional Indigenous American cultures. He was steadfast in his efforts to bring the Hopi message to the world via the United Nations.

As Banyacya explained in a 1961 letter, the Hopi began their efforts to address the leaders of the world at the House of Mica (UN) for three reasons: to look for their true white brother (Pahana or Bahana); to seek justice for all Indian brothers and sisters, and for all good people in this land; and "to warn the great leaders of the coming purification day which has been prophesied to come to this land of the red man when evil ones bring all life back to the day before the great flood, which destroyed all life in another world."

Mr. Banyacya's letter, which is reprinted in Rudolf Kaiser's book, *The Voice of the Great Spirit* (Shambhala, 1991), goes on to say "Our fore-fathers have all expressed their sincere faith that when the Hopi come before the leaders in the Glass House, at least two or three leaders or nations would hear and understand. For it is told that they should know these ancient instructions, too."

Over the years Mr. Banyacya said in many public forums that the people of the Earth have the opportunity and the responsibility to avoid the harsh consequences that the elders see as imminent. But each person and each nation must ask whether they are contributing to the destruction of the Earth, either through misguided action or indifference. And then things must be set straight.

Traditional Hopi elders began their active efforts to speak to world leaders at the UN in 1949. They were repeatedly turned away. Their efforts, however, began to weave a web of relationship and support. Thus, as other opportunities arose in recent decades, the elders spoke publicly of their understandings and their world view, and also of the importance of their delivering their message to the United Nations.

The Fire Clan Tablets

On December 13, 1990, a delegation of Hopi elders, greatly concerned about the events unfolding in the Persian Gulf prior to the start of the battle known as Desert Storm, made a pilgrimage to Santa Fe, New Mexico. There, in a meeting with Governor Bruce King and other state officials, they warned that humankind must return immediately to peaceful, Earth-honoring ways, or the world would soon come to a catastrophic end.

According to a report in the *Albuquerque Journal* the following day, the Hopi elders made their appeal in Santa Fe because it was the first European capitol among the Native people, founded in 1610, and thus had special significance for them. At the meeting, Martin Gashweseoma, keeper of the Hopi Fire Clan Stone Tablets, said that the Earth was getting "close to its last stages." After a twenty-minute discourse, translated into English by Hopi elder Thomas Banyacya, Gashweseoma untied a red and white scarf that encircled his waist and produced two small stone tablets.

According to the *Albuquerque Journal* report, one of the flat, dark brown stones was about the size of an index card; the other was about half that size. Both were about a quarter-inch thick and had symbols, lines, and other figures scratched on them.

Mr. Gashweseoma said the tablet has instructed generations of Hopi to watch for signs that the world is on a dangerous course. The final stage of this dangerous course, he said, can be identified by famine, sickness, earthquakes, natural disasters, and, finally, by the dangerous buildup of "weapons that are destructive to all mankind." Referring generally to events around the world, he said, "we are getting around to a dangerous period of our lives."

PHOTO 18. *Hopi Elder Martin Gashweseoma. Photo © 1993 by Wanelle Fitch.*

The sacred stone tablets are said to have been given to the Hopi by Massau'u, a messenger of Great Spirit, when the Hopi emerged from sanctuaries within the Earth at the start of the Fourth World, or the present epoch of history. The stones are rarely shown in public. According to the Hopi, there are other people around the world who were also given stone tablets by the Great Spirit. If the people all come together and follow the original instructions on these tablets, the world can move through the purification consciously, with minimal tumult and destruction.

The Final Stage

The text of Martin Gashweseoma's 1990 statement in Santa Fe was reprinted in the midwinter 1991 edition of *Akwesasne Notes*, the official publication of the Mohawk Nation. A portion of that text follows:

"I am the keeper of the sacred Fire Clan Tablet for the Hopi at the village of Hotevilla. This tablet represents our ancient title to this land, which has existed for many centuries before the arrival of Columbus, and has never been relinquished to this day. It has been entrusted to me under the highest authority, to be held until the last stage of our prophecies has been completed. The signs that we have entered that final stage are now clear.

"In fulfillment of my spiritual instructions, I have come to Santa Fe, the oldest European capital on our land, to offer the people of the United States of America, and all humanity, a final chance to collaborate with the forces of creation to purify our lives and restore peace to the world.

"Massau'u is both a real person and a manifestation of the Creator. We met him in person near the place where we built our mother village of Oraibi after a long migration to claim the land in his name. At that point he gave us permission to live here as caretakers, as well as the spiritual knowledge (*pitskwani*) by which to keep the forces of life in balance. This knowledge is implanted in our sacred stone tablets.

"But when the Europeans came they forced their foreign religions, culture and language upon our children, which brought great division among our people. As a result, today our young people are turning away from the basic law. They no longer understand it. They only understand the white man's law."

Mr. Gashweseoma said that because foreign religions, culture, and language have been forced upon the Indian children, "there is now hardly anyone fulfilling the sacred instructions and correctly performing the ceremonies essential to the Hopi way of life. There are still leaders from various clans who know of these instructions, which reveal their true purpose in life, but more and more they are turning away. This intrusion by outside forces, and the harmful effect on our function as caretakers of life, is the reason life on Earth is now so disturbed."

Planting a Seed of Realization

As he stood before the Santa Fe meeting, Mr. Gashweseoma said that each Hopi clan has a special function by which it helps hold life in balance. The Hopi clans were still carrying out their functions when the Europeans arrived. "We know these foreigners once had similar spiritual means for promoting life, with which they were supposed to bless the native peoples. But they had apparently misused their power. Most of the native people were forcibly stripped of their culture, language, and religious ceremonies, depriving them of their function as caretakers.

"[For these reasons] we bring our sacred stone tablets to the New Mexico state capital in Santa Fe...The Spanish, the Mexican, and the United States governments have all fought over someone else's land without consulting the original native peoples living on it, then created some kind of document to 'prove' their ownership. But what of the rights of the original native peoples? Who has the ability to look into this and see that the basic rights of the Hopi and other native people are restored?

"This is the key to the problem that threatens all life on Earth. If someone can uncover this information and bring it before the world, it might be possible to reverse the destruction of the native cultures that lies at the root of the destruction that now threatens our entire world."

In the 1990 book *Native American Prophecies,* journalist Scott Peterson interviewed a Hopi elder of the One Horn Society in Hotevilla, who offered his insight on the critical issue of land title: "The ultimate philosophical foundation for the cultural values that exist in Hopi culture is that nobody owns the land. You have the right to use it. If you have the energy, the motivation, and the ability to provide the necessary food or whatever from working this Earth, and take care of it, you have the right to use it. That's all. You can't claim this acre is yours, or that two acres."

"The stone tablets only really mean that this is a path of life and instruction for people to exist with the elements of the Earth. If you interpret it this way, that tablet only means that whenever people get together and figure out a way to establish a situation where they can live in harmony, then the path will have been followed."

At the 1990 meeting in Santa Fe, in addition to speaking about the human relationship with the land, Martin Gashweseoma made several other telling points: "The great powers of the modern world need to realize that if they are to escape the punishment that lies ahead, what they are doing to native peoples around the world must be corrected. Those who accumulated power at the expense of the native peoples think they have a God-given right, but in doing so they are increasing the threat to all life. And although they now recognize that threat, they are powerless to reverse it by any means unless they stop preying upon the native peoples.

"We came here to plant the seed of this realization, which could turn the course of all humanity away from disaster. Because our true original land title is essential to our role in holding this land and life in balance, we have never compromised that title by signing a treaty with the United States government. We have never given it authority to destroy our culture and take our land, nor have the other original native peoples. Yet this is being done here and throughout the world.

"They are cutting our land into small allotments, confiscating our livestock, and allowing the land to be stripped of its mineral resources. Underground water is being depleted and the land is drying up. Open pit uranium mines are polluting the area with radioactivity, causing the birth of many deformed babies. This shows what is happening to indigenous people around the world.

"But as the Great Purification foretold in our tradition materializes, [the abusers] will get kicked around. They will find themselves disrespected everywhere, just as they have disrespected others, and their power will collapse. Soon they will see how little power and authority they really have.

"We hope they will heed our warning for their own sake, and for the sake of the native peoples who want nothing more than to rule themselves peacefully without being dictated to by anyone else. Part of the commission we received from the Creator through Massau'u is to sound this warning to the world.

"We Hopi know our true white brother is to come and help us. He has a stone tablet representing his own title and power within the Creator's plan. By placing it together with our Fire Clan Tablet, he may call upon the natural forces to purify the world. If the task of purification is left to these natural forces, we may be all wiped out. So it is up to all people to purify themselves voluntarily."

"The severe problems that face not only humanity, but every form of life on Earth, serve to warn that the time of destruction is at hand. That is why I act now to call world attention to the true nature of aboriginal land title, which alone holds the key to world peace. Hopi land title is based on our agreement with the Creator, the true owner of the land, through our meeting with Massau'u, to serve as its caretakers. This requires genuine knowledge of the pattern through which people can live together in peace without relying on the use of force. This way of life can continue forever."

The efforts of traditional Hopi elders to continue living by the original instructions are often undermined or thwarted by various other factions within the Hopi nation, factions often influenced by commercial or governmental interests. Of particular note, after the 1990 Santa Fe meeting, the stone tablets entrusted to Martin Gashweseoma as their official custodian and as the sole determiner of their use, were taken from him by his own relatives who were members of the US-government–affiliated Hopi Tribal Council. They took the tablets on the grounds that Mr. Gashweseoma should not have shown them in Santa Fe. Mr. Gashweseoma said he sees this taking as part of the imbalance and chaos of which Hopi Prophecy fortells.

The Return of Pahana

According to Robert Boissiere's 1990 book, *The Return of Pahana: A Hopi Myth*, Pahana, or Bahana, is the name given by the Hopi to the mythic brother of an original pair of twins whose role was to insure harmony in the world. Pahana, who was of white coloration (the word also means "white man"), decided to leave the original people to investigate the rest of the world. He headed east. As a sort of passport, he took with him one set of the original stone tablets that had been given to the Hopi by Massau'u, the god-guardian of Earth.

To this day, Boissiere writes, most Hopi believe neither Pahana nor his tablets have returned. However, Hopi legend relates that Pahana will return bearing his tablets when his power is needed to reestablish balance and harmony in the world. Furthermore, many traditional Hopi believe that this time is imminent:

Boissiere concludes his discussion of Pahana with an assessment of the importance of similar "myths of return" in cultures around the world: "Of all the Mesoamerican myths that have resurfaced from the past, the Quetzalcoatl-Pahana myth of the returning savior is the most widely recognized. It not only underlies the entire esoteric and mystic past of native America, but it is also astonishingly similar to the Old World myth of the Second Coming, which had its sources in Chaldean, Sumerian, Babylonian, Assyrian, Greek, Egyptian, and Roman mythology."

Chapter Eight

Messengers at
the House of Mica

L ess than one year after the Santa Fe meeting, Hopi messenger
    Thomas Banyacya traveled to the far eastern shore of Turtle Island
to knock for a final time at the door to the House of Mica, the gleaming
glass building that houses the United Nations in the heart of New York
City. Arriving at the UN in October, 1991 Banyacya was joined and
supported in his pilgrimage by a large network of people from both
indigenous and technological cultures.

Mr. Banyacya entered UN grounds ceremonially through the
Western gate of the House of Mica, which is usually locked. He carried
in his hand the eagle prayer feather that had been given to him in 1948
by the Hopi elders of that day. As Banyacya entered the UN, his core
support circle of Hopi elders sat in their kiva at Hotevilla, embraced by
the Earth, holding vigil.

After walking through the Western gate Mr. Banyacya presented
the sacred feather, and a letter, to UN official John Washburn in the
Secretary General's Office. This was the start of the fourth and final
knock of the Hopi at the House of Mica.

However, it was not until a year later, in December, 1992, that the
Hopi got an answer from the nation states of the world, and even then

it was only a partial answer. The response to the knocks was half-hearted. In essence, the UN said "the door will open, but not formally. Your speakers may speak, but we won't pay much attention."

Half A Circle

In early 1992 indigenous leaders from around the globe, including Thomas Banyacya, again journeyed at their own expense to New York City to take part in a meeting that would mark the 50th anniversary of the UN Declaration of Human Rights, a seminal document. The coalition of indigenous delegates gathered in the offices of the American Friends Service on East 34th Street, perched on a knoll just above the sprawling, palatial House of Mica. There they prepared to meet with UN officials.

Then on December 10, 1992—the morning after a total eclipse of the Moon, and the same day that Guatemalan Indian activist Rigoberta Menchu received the Nobel Peace Prize in Stockholm, Sweden—the UN opened its door a crack. Representatives from 20 indigenous nations spoke at a convocation in the UN General Assembly Hall. It was the first time in history that indigenous people of the Americas were allowed to speak in the main chamber of the global organization which makes its home base on the very soil—Turtle Island—that indigenous people say they have been entrusted to caretake.

However, the UN's General Assembly formally adjourned beforehand. Only about one-third of the delegates remained, in unofficial capacity, to hear the messages of the Earth-based peoples. That audience dwindled dramatically as the presentations continued. The

PHOTO 19. *The House of Mica, United Nations Headquarters in New York City with its distinctive glass façade—which gleams like the mineral mica in the desert sunshine. (UN Photo 104 713 SAW LWIN).*

mass media likewise turned its collective back on the gatherings and the messages. Scarcely a word of the traditional elders' message was reported to the public.

One speaker at the UN convocation was Chief Oren Lyons, Faithkeeper for the Onondaga, Haudenausenee (Iroquois Six Nations), and a professor at the State University of New York, Buffalo. In his remarks, Chief Lyons reminded world leaders of the history of relations among peoples of the technological cultures and those of the natural cultures: "The catastrophes we have suffered at the hands of our brothers from across the sea have been unremitting and inexcusable. It has crushed our peoples and nations down through the past five centuries."

Lyons spoke of the "Original Instructions," natural laws that his people feel were given to them by the Creator, including the idea of respecting "all things" as part of the sacred circle—or hoop—of life. He also spoke of Indian prophecies. "We are the generation with the responsibility and option to choose the path with a future for our children. We must join hands with the rest of creation, and speak of common sense, responsibility, brotherhood, and peace."

The prophetic idea that a time would come when the earth would pass through a period of chaos and cleansing is common in Native American nations. According to a number of ancient Native seers, and as articulated frequently by the late Chippewa visionary Sun Bear, this time could be identified by, among other things, environmental desecration, extermination of various plants and animals, great wars, massive storms, upheavals of the earth, and general fear and confusion among people who had lost their connection with Spirit.

According to many of these prophecies, as the chaos intensified, the world would be shaken in various ways to bring about purification and then, eventually, returned to balance. Balance would come when the two-leggeds (human beings) remembered that they have a responsibility to live in stewardship of the earth, which makes all life possible. Many people would awaken and realize the fundamental importance of taking care of Mother Earth and using her gifts—the plants, animals, waters, and minerals—with thanksgiving, praise, and appreciation, always asking permission and offering something in return for whatever is taken.

We Made a Sacred Covenant

In the half-circle of the UN's General Assembly hall, on the night of Dec. 10, 1992, Hopi elder Thomas Banyacya was the final speaker. As reported at the time by correspondent Valerie Taliman of *Indian Country Today*, Mr. Banyacya's presentation was preceded by three loud shouts, sounded by Iroquois Faithkeeper Oren Lyons. His shouts were an announcement to Great Spirit, and to the assembly, that all should listen closely to a message of spiritual importance.

Despite the deserted delegate seats in the General Assembly hall that night, by all accounts Thomas Banyacya delivered an eloquent oration. In an interview several weeks after that night, he emphasized that while he was a messenger, it was never intended that he deliver the long-prophesied message for the Hopi. "My job was to try and help open the door," he said, "so one of our spiritual people would be able to speak, not me."

Even though the UN faltered at that time in its chance to open its doors wide and complete the circle by actively and respectfully con-sidering the words of the intended spokesperson of the Hopi, Mr. Banyacya blessed the assembly. He sprinkled corn meal around the podium, prayed in his native Hopi language, called on the Four Directions and ancestral spirits. Then he said what he could.

"My name is Banyacya of the Wolf, Fox, and Coyote Clans," he said, "and I am a member of the Hopi sovereign nation. Hopi in our language means a peaceful, kind, gentle, truthful people. The tradi-tional Hopi follow the spiritual path that was given to us by Massau'u, the Great Spirit. We made a sacred covenant to follow his life plan at all times, which includes the responsibility of taking care of this land and life for his divine purpose.

"Our goals are not to gain political control, monetary wealth or military power, but rather to pray and to promote the welfare of all living beings and to preserve the world in a natural way. We still have our ancient sacred stone tablets and spiritual religious societies, which are the foundations of the Hopi way of life.

"In 1948 all traditional Hopi spiritual leaders met and spoke of things I felt strongly were of great importance to all people. They selected four interpreters to carry their message, of which I am the only one living today. My mission has been to open the doors of this Great

House of Mica to native peoples. The elders said to knock four times, and this commitment has now been filled.

"At the meeting in 1948, Hopi leaders—80, 90 and even 100 years old—explained that the Creator made the first world in perfect balance where humans spoke one language. But humans turned away from moral and spiritual principles. They misused their spiritual powers for selfish purposes. They did not follow nature's rules. Eventually the world was destroyed by the sinking of land and the separation of land by what you would call major earthquakes. Many died and only a small handful survived.

"Then this handful of people came into the second world. They repeated their mistakes and the world was destroyed by freezing which you call the great Ice Age.

"The few survivors of this time entered then into the third world. That world lasted a long time and as in previous worlds, the people spoke only one language. The people invented many machines and conveniences of high technology, some of which have not yet been seen in this age. They even had spiritual powers that they used for good. They also gradually turned away from natural laws and pursued only material things, and finally only gambled while they ridiculed spiritual principles. No one stopped them from this course and the world was destroyed by the great flood that many nations still recall in their ancient history or in their religions.

"The elders said that, again, only small groups escaped and came to this fourth world where we now live. Now our world is in terrible shape again today, even though the Great Spirit gave us different languages and sent us to the four corners of the world and told us to take care of the Earth and all that is in it.

"The Hopi knew that humans would develop many powerful technologies that would be abused. In this century we have seen the First World War and the Second World War in which the predicted gourd of ashes, which you call the atomic bomb, fell from the sky with great destruction. Many thousands of people were destroyed in Hiroshima and Nagasaki. For many years there has been great fear and danger of World War Three. The Hopi believe the Persian Gulf War (Desert Storm) was the beginning of World War Three, but it was stopped, and the worst weapons of war were not used. This is now a time to weigh the choices for our future. We do have a choice. If you, the nations of this Earth, create another great war, the Hopi believe we humans will burn ourselves to death with ashes. That's why the spiritual elders stress strongly that the United Nations fully open the door for native spiritual leaders as soon as possible.

"Nature itself does not speak with a voice that we can easily understand. Neither can the animals and birds we are threatening with extinction talk to us. Who in this world can speak for nature and the spiritual energy that creates and flows through all life?

"In every continent are human beings who are like you, but who have not separated themselves from the land and from nature. It is through their voices that nature can speak to us. You have heard those voices and many messages from the four corners of the world today. I have studied comparative religion and I think in your own nations and cultures you have knowledge of the consequences of living out of balance with nature and spirit. The native peoples of the world have seen and spoken to you about the destruction of their lives and homelands, the ruination of nature and the desecration of their sacred sites. It is time the United Nations used its rules to investigate these occurrences and to stop them now.

"The Hopi and all original native people hold the land in balance by prayer, fasting, and performing ceremonies. Our Spiritual Elders still hold the land in the Western Hemisphere in balance for all living beings, including humans.

"The United Nations stands on our native homeland. The United Nations talks about human rights, equality and justice and yet the native people have never had a real opportunity to speak to this assembly until today. It should be the mission of your nations and this assembly to use your power and rules to examine and work to cure the damage people have done to this Earth and to each other. Hopi Elders know that was your mission and they wait to see whether you will act on it now.

"I hope that all members of this assembly that know the spiritual way will not just talk about it, but in order to have real peace and harmony, that they will follow what it says across the United Nations wall: 'They will beat their swords into plowshares and study war no more.' Let us together do that now!"

Storm of the Century

"It's going to be worse," Mr. Banyacya later observed about the cleansing of the planet. "We pray every day that it won't be that way, but if the United Nations doesn't listen to the traditional indigenous leaders from the Four Directions, it's going to be a lot worse. If we don't listen, nature will make us."

As a whole, the UN and the world paid scant attention to the people of the Four Directions on December 10, 1992. The door opened only a grudging crack in response to the four knocks of the Hopi. Mother Nature, however, chose this pivotal moment to emphasize the fourth knock of the people of the Four Directions with a resounding knock of her own.

As Banyacya finished his speech that night, and as the indigenous leaders departed the technological wonderland in and around the great House of Mica, a massive storm slammed the metropolis of New York, and the whole east coast of the nation–state now set upon Turtle Island. From the Carolinas to Maine, skies and seas flashed to life. Fire pinpointed a building on East 34th St., just blocks from where the UN perches upon the fabled island—acquired through an infamous transaction between the Manhattan tribe and a company of European merchants.

High winds, wild seas, and torrential sheets of rain and sleet battered the city for two ruinous days. The hurricane-force storm shut down the city: closed the airports, flooded the subways, and swamped FDR Drive and much of the East Side. There the UN sits shining by the spoiled waters of the East River. Just a few hundred yards away, across streaming rivers of toxic air and water, sprawls the spoiled industrial shore of Queens. The gleaming glass walls of the House of Mica, and the gray, fuming smoke stacks of its industrial culture sit juxtaposed—within easy view of each other, albeit through an infernal and omnipresent haze.

As the great storm raged, the subfloors of the UN building itself were flooded, shutting down the heating and ventilation systems. UN headquarters was closed, and scuba divers searched about for damage outside on FDR Drive.

"The storm was absolutely wild," recalls Rev. Betsy Stang, who attended the gathering. "Several of us encouraged the indigenous elders to do what they could about the storm. Finally, Grandfather Thomas called a Four Directions prayer circle in one of the meeting rooms at the UN. He blessed the circle with corn meal, and invited people of all the colors and religions to pray together. Within 40 minutes the storm had abated. A lot of people—a lot of UN officials—were able to put two and two together. Let's just say that all of this was noticed; it made an impression."

Still, the UN appeared to say to the native leaders, "it's very nice that you're here for a visit, but we are very busy with other concerns." If the official UN representatives had listened throughout the day on December 10, what they would have heard from the many indigenous spokespeople was a mixture of well-earned anger at centuries of systematic injustice, but ultimately a message of peace. Native speakers called for justice, and they called for people to return to the original instructions of the Creator: 'to remember that we exist in a universe of living Spirit, and to remember that all things are related in the Sacred Hoop of life. Respect and harmony must prevail.' The words of the delegates were simple and severe, and also touched with compassion and hope for better relations with each other and the planet we all share.

In the wild days that followed the half-hearted UN designation of 1993 as the "Year of the World's Indigenous Peoples," major news outlets breathed not a word of the earth peoples or their message. Reporters occupied themselves instead with what *The New York Times* labeled "a storm of the century," and with pending actions in Sarajevo and Somalia, where the madness had come full term.

The Cry Of the Earth

Shortly after his speech at the UN, Mr. Banyacya called Betsy Stang at the Wittenberg Center for Alternative Resources, and strongly encouraged her to help him open the door to the UN. She brought his entreaty before the Committee for Giving of Thanks to the First Nations, a group within New York's Cathedral of St. John the Divine. The committee, including members Beatriz Beltran and Carina Courtright, recognized the need. As 1993 got underway they decided to see if they could help create another opportunity for the Hopi and Spiritual Elders from the Four Directions to be heard at the UN.

They spearheaded a year of negotiations with UN officials and the Hopi. "It took a lot of hard work from lots of people," Ms. Courtright later commented, "but ultimately it was truly miraculous that it happened." Native elders were enthusiastic about the opportunity, while the UN bureaucracy was reluctant. Finally, with the help of many others, including the special assistance of Stoyan Ganev, President of the 47th General Assembly, and Leia Boutros-Ghali, wife of the UN's Secretary General, all obstacles were overcome and arrangements were made for what might be termed a "fifth knock on the door"—a conference at UN headquarters entitled The Cry of the Earth, The Legacy of the First Nations. The conference was set for November 22, 1993.

Seven delegations, all from North American indigenous nations, including the Hopi, spoke at Cry of the Earth, which was sponsored by the Crescentera Foundation, with the assistance of the Wittenberg Center for Alternative Resources. Although the gathering was not an official UN conference, it was cosponsored by the Mexican Mission to the UN, the US Mission to the UN, and the UN Centre for Human Rights.

According to Ms. Courtright, Director of the Crescentera Foundation, the purpose of the conference was to allow Native American spokespeople an opportunity to articulate their spiritual visions and prophecies regarding the condition of the earth and her people. It was also

THE CRY OF THE EARTH

PHOTO 20. *The Seven Fires Wampum Belt is displayed at the Cry of the Earth conference by Algonquin elder William Commanda (center), and his helpers Frank Decontie (l) and Eddie Decontie (r). (UN Photo 184764/J.Issac).*

hoped that the conference would open the doors of the UN to the concerns and contributions of indigenous peoples from around the planet.

Thus finally—after forty-five years of steady effort—traditional elders of the Hopi Nation delivered their prophetic message to the leaders of the world at United Nations headquarters in New York City on November 22, 1993. In so doing they say they fulfilled the instructions that were given to them by the Creator at the beginning of this epoch of history, called *Tewaquachi*, the Fourth World, by their reckoning.

A delegation of four Hopi elders, led by Martin Gashweseoma and including Thomas Banyacya, was joined and supported at the United Nation's Cry of the Earth conference by 24 other spiritual elders from "the Four Directions," representing the Maya, Huichol, Lakota, Miqmac, Haudenausenee (Six Nations Iroquois Confederacy), and Mamuwinini (Algonquin) Nations of North America.

At UN headquarters, the elders delivered an explicit warning that the time of purification spoken of in their traditions is already in progress, and likely to intensify in the future unless people return to follow the instructions of the Creator: to live simply, in respect and harmony with all things. For hour after hour they presented their prophecies, handed down orally since antiquity, regarding the ecological, spiritual, and ethical crises confronting humanity today.

The unprecedented gathering of spiritual elders came near the end of the UN's "International Year of the World's Indigenous Peoples," and just weeks before the UN voted to designate a "Decade of the World's Indigenous Peoples," from 1995 to 2004. The landmark conference took place in the Economic and Social Council chamber at UN headquarters before 350 observers, including some UN delegates and officials. The event was opened by S.R. Insanally, President of the 48th Session of the UN General Assembly, and was closed by Ibrahima Fall, Assistant Secretary General for Human rights.

The Time of Withering Fruit

At the conference delegates from seven Native American Nations spoke of their traditional visions and prophecies, including Onondaga Chief Leon Shenandoah, Todadaho of the Iroquois Six Nations: Arvol Looking Horse, 19th Generation Keeper of the Sacred White Buffalo Calf Woman Pipe for the Lakota Nation; Traditional Algonquin Elder

William Commanda, Keeper of the Primstaven and the Seven Fires Prophecy Wampum Belt for all the people: David Gehue, Spiritual Counselor of the MiqMaq Nation; Doñ Santiago Itza Can, Priest of the Tulum Circle, Maya Nation; Marcos Torres Carillo, Mara'akame of the Huichol Nation; and Martin Gashweseoma, Caretaker, Sovereign Hopi Nation.

Within the House of Mica, the native speakers called for unity, and agreed that we have already entered the time of "withering fruit"—a time when erratic weather patterns, earth movements, starvation, violence, and war have come to pass with great frequency and intensity, as the Grandmothers and Grandfathers of antiquity had foretold.

The elders also agreed that this is a time for all people to return to spirit, and to heal the heart. Various speakers identified keys to this healing process: the Iroquois spoke of love for one another and respect for all of nature; the Algonquin spoke of forgiveness and sacrifice; the Mic Mac spoke of the importance of honesty, respect, caring and sharing.

After the conference, representatives from the Native delegations met privately with Secretary General Boutros Boutros-Ghali, to open dialogue about further including indigenous peoples in UN affairs.

Messages From The Four Directions

Over twenty-eight traditional Native American spiritual elders spoke at the Cry of the Earth conference at the House of Mica on November 22, 1993. The full proceedings were recorded on videotape (see General Resources). What follows is a partial text of four presentations:

Martin Gashweseoma, Hopi Caretaker of the Sovereign Hopi Nation for the Great Spirit, Massau'u:

"We are now living in the fourth and final world of the Hopi. We are at a most critical time in human history. It is a crossroads at which the outcome of our actions will decide the fate of all life on earth.

"At the beginning of this fourth world the Hopi were told to watch for specific signs which would mark this crucial period and were also given instructions for actions to avoid the annihilation of this world, and for life to continue.

"The instructions included a directive to travel to a great House of Mica (glass) which would be built on the distant eastern shore of this continent where leaders of the earth's nations would gather. The Hopi were instructed to knock on the door of this house in order to deliver their message to those gathered there. If refused, they were to knock again until they had done so four times.

"Since 1949 the Hopi have knocked at the door of the United Nations. Last December was the fourth and final time they would do so. Having received an invitation from the United Nations, this historic gathering which Hopi spiritual leaders have requested is the final fulfillment of these instructions.

"All the things that were to come were told to the first people in Oraibi by the first people that came from the under-world. And these understandings or prophecies, as they are also called, were continued—passed on from generation to generation from that day to this.

"The people were told of another race of people who would come to this land and claim it as their own land. We were told not to accept anything these people would offer to us, but it will tempt us and be hard to resist. They would be intelligent and the inventors of many things. Now we realize that these people are the light-skinned people, the Bahanas.

"We were told of something that would come that would be pulled by animals, meaning wagons or carts. And ones that would run very fast, meaning automobiles and other motorized vehicles. We were told of the land being cut up by long roads and fences, and of highways that would be built in the sky. And that women would adopt male clothing. And that the secret of women, with clothing covered, would no longer be secret, but be revealed and exposed.

"When this happens, all the world leaders and all the people will be corrupted and will not know whom to look to for direction to correct this corruption. When all this happens, it will mean that we are all nearing the end. Then the wars will come about like powerful winds, and will spread from country to country and bring purification or destruction to this world. The more we turn away from the instructions of the Great Spirit, Massau'u, the more signs we see in the form of earthquakes, floods, drought, fires, tornadoes, as Nature makes ready her revenge. All of this will happen at one time along with the wars and corruption. We see this now as young children become angry, killing each other and their parents. They show no respect. We are all corrupt.

"If this purification does not materialize then the world will turn over four times and will leave only ants here to start a new life. Before people came to this world they were sick, just as today we are sick from all this corruption. Now we are seeking a way to solve our present situation. This is the last world, we are not going anywhere from here. If we destroy this, the highest world, which is like heaven, we will be given no other chances.

"Let us consider this matter seriously so that this world is not destroyed, so that we can continue to live and save this land and life for the generations to come."

David Gehue of the MiqMac Nation, Spiritual Councilor: "From the Eastern Door: we are in the final stages of the shaking of the earth, when the Great Spirit takes the Earth in both hands and shakes it violently.

"Just this year (1993) the opening of the eastern door took place in Cape Spear, Newfoundland, Canada, the furthest eastern point in North America. The circle of the Medicine Wheel is now complete. The Wabanaki People (People of the Morning Light) have joined the circle. We have joined under the following philosophy: 'Heal yourself—you help to heal the family, the family helps to heal the community, the community helps to heal the nation, the nations helps to heal the world.'

"All the prophecies from the other nations now coincide and complement each other. It is time for us all to stop blaming one another, heal from our wounds, and move forward—for the survival of the world as we know it is in our hands.

"We must seek out and absorb the wisdom of our elders and use it for the betterment of others. The Great Spirit left a clear and legible path in eastern North America with petroglyphs and natural monuments. This knowledge is kept under guard by our elders and only entrusted to those native people who abide by the natural laws of the Great Spirit: respect, honesty, sharing, and caring. Without each one of these the others do not exist.

"It is now time for moms, dads, grandmothers, grandfathers, and children to get involved in the healing of our world. Make it your business, too."

Audrey Shehandoah, Clan Mother, Onondaga Nation, Six Nations Iroquois Confederacy:

"I, myself, have a very quick message from the women of indigenous peoples. I would say, from the women of this Earth, our Mother Earth is crying from abuse and disrespect. And the mothers of the nations of this Earth are also crying. I'm speaking about the mothers who have not lost their relationship to our Mother Earth. I'm speaking about the mothers and women who are still connected to the things of Earth, life-giving Mother Earth. I'm talking about the mothers who, in spite of all the stress in today's times are hanging on and really doing battle so that our traditions might live on. That these true ways that were given to our people will live on. That our grandchildren, our great-grandchildren, and our children seven generations into the future will have clean water, will have water to drink, will have clean food to take into their bodies, so that there will be life.

"We are in very, very difficult times, and it becomes an individual kind of thing for people to change their lifestyle in order for the things going on here on this Earth to change. We cannot wait for large amounts of money from huge committees or organizations to make the changes for us.

"In our nation, the women have a very noble and respectful place in our society, and the women are in the forefront of keeping our traditions, of keeping our way of life that was given to us in the beginning of our time. This is the way that we are told it should be. Our leadership does not make decisions without consulting the women within our nations. Because the mothers, the women, are life givers themselves. So, as the

Earth is crying, the mothers of the nations are bleeding in their hearts and crying also for the future generations."

Chief Leon Shenandoah, Tadadaho, Onandaga Nation, Six Nations Iroquois Confederacy:

"It is prophesied in our Instructions that the end of the world will be near when the trees start dying from the tops down. That's what the maples are doing now. Our Instructions say the time will come when there will be no corn, when nothing will grow in the garden, when the water will be unfit to drink... We were instructed to carry love for one another, and to show great respect for all the beings of the earth.

"In our ways, spiritual consciousness is the highest form of politics. We must live in harmony with the natural world and recognize that excessive exploitation can only lead to our own destruction. We cannot trade the welfare of our future generations for profit now.

"We must stand together, the four sacred colors of man, as the one family that we are, in the interest of peace. We must abolish nuclear and conventional weapons of war... We must raise leaders of peace. We must unite the religions of the world as a spiritual force strong enough to prevail in peace. We (human beings) are a spiritual energy that is thousands of times stronger than nuclear energy. Our energy is the combined will of all people with the spirit of the natural world, to be of one body, one heart, and one mind for peace."

You Must Find Your Own Way

In meetings that followed the Cry of the Earth conference, some attendees asked the traditional elders "how do I know what I need to do? Who can I ask to learn more about your ways?"

Manuel Hoyongowa, grandson of the late Hopi Grandfather David Monongye, responded "Don't look to us for your answers. Our way is not The Way. Look into your own heart, and come as close to the voice of your own heart as you can so you can hear the voice of your own heritage. You must figure it out, and see through which tradition it will speak. You must find your own way."

Despite the fact that the Cry of the Earth conference offered the bread-and-butter of mass media—high drama, colorful visuals, and vivid soundbites—the media once again turned its back on the Earth peoples. Scarcely a word of the elders' message was reported to the public. Still, even though the global media paid no attention, when Cry of the Earth was complete Carina Courtright offered this assessment of the gathering: "They (the elders) felt this was incredibly important, for it was the first time spiritual elders from all over North America got together to speak their prophecies in a public forum. It was a real re-bonding of indigenous people here on Turtle Island."

According to Miqmac Spiritual Counselor David Gehue, the Cry of the Earth was clearly a fulfillment of the final prophecies. "They all coincide," he observed. "They all say the same thing basically, sometimes in different words or with different stories, but they all lead to the same thing.

"The understanding that comes from the Miqmaq is that all the Wabanaki (People of the Morning Light) were the first ones encountered by the Europeans. They got to us first, and we were absolutely bombarded. That bombardment caused 500 years of depletion and destruction of our traditions and ceremonies. But now they are coming back. It was predicted a long time ago that we would finally come back into the circle to complete it. Now we have done it. We have completed the Sacred Hoop by opening the Eastern Door, which was the final door of all the directions that had to be opened.

"So now, what comes next?" Mr. Gehue asked rhetorically. "The elders have been saying for a long, long time, that the world is going to go faster. Things have always happened; there have always been big storms, and earthquakes, floods, and fires, but now they are happening fast, and it's accelerating. It's going to go a lot faster. Because of this, it's real important that we start to slow down.

"Heal the inner self: you have to be open for that. You have to master you—your weaknesses, your fears, and your rages. You have to master that. You have to make sure that you are thinking clearly, and feeling clearly.

The key for all the people in North America is: get to know who you are. Get rid of all your emotional and spiritual garbage—hate, fear, fire and brimstone, all that junk. The Creator is not standing somewhere

PHOTO 21. *Traditional Elders of the Four Directions meet with UN Secretary General Boutros Boutros Ghali in his office at the conclusion of the Cry of the Earth. Photo © 1993 by Wanelle Fitch.*

with a big stick ready to beat you. You can be who you are. You need to be who you are. That's the bottom line."

At the conclusion of Cry of the Earth, the elders of the Four Directions were invited into the offices of then UN Secretary General, Boutros Boutros Ghali. After the group posed for a photo, the Secretary General asked the elders if there was anything he could do for them.

David Gehue said "Yes, we want a seat here in this forum, the House of Mica that stands upon our homeland, Turtle Island. This is what we want."

This Is What the Hopi Say

During a telephone interview two months after the UN Cry of the Earth conference, Thomas Banyacya said he was at last satisfied that the Hopi had fulfilled their ancient instructions to deliver a message at the House of Mica. "Yes," he said, "this has been fulfilled. The instructions told me that first I must meet with all the Hopi pueblos here, which I did, and then also to check and compare our knowledge with other native people, which I did. For six years I went back and forth across this country, and to every Province in Canada, the Yukon in Alaska, El Salvador, and Puerto Rico. And the people there know these things. They had similar prophecies and messages. They all said it was going to be hard, but it finally happened that the United Nations opened its doors to native people. So that part is fulfilled. That part is good."

"At first many people just laughed and called me crazy and all that," Mr. Banyacya recalled. "But the Hopi elders said that eventually the world's problems are going to be so great that every nation's peoples are going to be looking for survival. That's what's happening right now, and I think many people have begun to understand what we have been saying.

"I hope that out of this spreading of the Hopi message and warning many nations will really do something for themselves. We are not going to save anyone. We're just delivering a message from Spirit that was given to us. These nations, they are the ones that are supposed to do something. The people of the United States and Canada and elsewhere, it's up to them to correct the troubles and see if they can straighten out the many problems.

"This is the only country we have, the only home we have," Mr. Banyacya said. "The Great Spirit based us here to take care of this land and life for Him through prayer, meditations, ceremonies, and rituals, and to lead a simple life close to the Earth. That's what we have been doing. These governments talk all the time about human rights, equality, justice, and all those things, but they have never done anything for the native people. Never.

"So it's time that they do that, live up to their talk, otherwise nature is going to take over. Earthquakes, flooding, destruction by volcanic eruptions, tidal waves, things like that—nature's going to keep warning us.

"The Hopi prophecy says that there may be three nations there [at the UN] that decide they finally have to check on these things so that they will not face the terrible punishment that people are going to face if they don't correct these things right now. That's why we are doing this, trying to give everybody a chance to correct themselves and to correct the wrongdoings right now."

When they spoke at the UN in 1993, the elders gave world leaders "four days, four weeks, four months" to respond to their message with sincere action. That deadline elapsed on April 23, 1994 with no official response from any world governments. One week later, though, the US government did host an unprecedented White House conference with leaders from tribal governments sanctioned by the US Bureau of

Indian Affairs. At that White House meeting President William Jefferson Clinton heartily endorsed the move to establish gambling casinos on Indian Reservations as a means of economic development. Many traditional spiritual elders not only oppose gambling, but say that, according to their historical understandings, gambling was one of the profane factors that brought on the great cleansing flood at the end of the third world.

"Now it's up to them, or up to the people," Mr. Banyacya said in a telephone interview. "We have been sending letters and telling people all this time, so it's up to them now. If the people don't correct, change, stop all these things, then the purification's really going to clean this mess up. Otherwise maybe only a handful of people will survive. That is what the Hopi say."

Note: Grandfather Thomas Banyacya died on February 6, 1999 at a hospital in Keam's Canyon, Arizona—just east of his home in Kykotsmovi. He was 89 years old. His life's work and message were simple yet still unfathomable to most of the modern world. As he saw it, the problems of our society are rooted in human thinking clouded by attachments to the world of material comforts—materialism. To solve these problems we have only to reawaken spiritually to our innate spiritual bond with all of life as our relations, and to all people as one human race, albeit with different ideas and different colored skins. Banyacya was firm in his conviction that a simple, spiritually focused lifestyle is the only way appropriate in these times of increasing wars and natural disasters—all of which he viewed as brought on by this fundamental error in human thinking. He prayed that, as the prophecies indicated, one or two nations at the UN would hear the Hopi Message and respond.

In July of the year 2000, the UN's Economic and Social Council adopted by consensus a resolution establishing a Permanent Forum for Indigenous Issues. This was an unprecedented event in the international community. Indigenous representatives, not only representatives of UN Member States, will, for the first time, participate in a high-level forum in the United Nations system—though not directly in the General Assembly. Consequently, the resolution is not full recognition, but does constitute a major step in that direction

Four years after the Cry of the Earth conference, the UN Commission on Human Rights sent a Special Rapporteur (reporter) across the United Sates, including a visit to Arizona. He came to look into issues of civil and political rights brought forward by Native American groups, including the Hopi and their specific concerns about Black Mesa, which is a colossal, Byzantine and ominous thicket of related issues for America. The issues central to Black Mesa tie together nuclear power, coal, water, matters of indigenous sovereignty, and the spiritual–energetic balance of the continent.

The visit of the Special Rapporteur settled or resolved nothing, but it did bring a host of indigenous concerns to official light within the structure of the United Nations. From this more may develop. In the 1998 interim report on this investigation, submitted by Mr. Abdelfattah Amor, he recommended that in the larger legal sphere of the US "Native Americans' system of values and traditions should be fully recognized, particularly as regards the concept of collective property rights, inalienability of sacred sites and secrecy with regard to their location." That is far more acknowledgement and respect than native concerns have to date received in national or international forums. It may mark a change.

Echoes of the Elders' Message

In the months surrounding the time that the traditional elders from the Four Directions delivered their messages at UN Headquarters (late 1993 and early 1994), four news reports echoed their warnings:

- Worldwatch Institute reported that "bird populations are declining or collapsing all over the world. Of the 9,600 species of birds known worldwide, more than 6,000 are in decline. Of these 1,000 appear headed for extinction.

- The UN Food and Agriculture Office reported that all 17 of the great fishing grounds on the planet have reached or exceeded their natural limits, and that nine of these primary fishing grounds are threatened with total species collapse.

- The State of the World 1994 report asserted that the world has passed its biological limit: "As a result of our population size, consumption patterns, and choice of technology, we have surpassed the planet's carrying capacity and the world is experiencing a massive slowdown in the growth of food production. More hungry times lie ahead."

• Researchers at Oregon State University discovered a clear link between increased ultraviolet radiation caused by the thinning of the ozone layer, and an ominous decline and mutation in the worldwide population of frogs, toads, and other insect-eating amphibians. The researchers said that acid rain and other forms of pollution are also suspected factors. By the year 2000, the US Wildlife Service set out to probe more deeply into why—around the world—biologists were continuing to find more and more frogs, toads, and salamanders with missing or extra limbs, oversized jaws, or without eyes. As the massive study got underway, the researchers said that for people the frogs are serving in the same way canaries once served miners—warning us with their deaths of a toxic and ultimately uninhabitable environment.

Chapter Nine

White Buffalo
and Whirling Rainbow

"Central to White Buffalo Woman's message, to all native spirituality, is the understanding that the Great Spirit lives in all things, enlivens all forms, and gives energy to all things in all realms of creation—including Earthly life.

Ancient teachings call us to turn primary attention to the Sacred Web of life, of which we are a part and with which we are so obviously entangled. This quality of attention—paying attention to the whole—is called among my people 'holiness'."

— Brooke Medicine Eagle

Nine months after the Hopi and other traditional elders delivered their message at the House of Mica, as if they had initiated a birth process with their words, a legend became a living reality: a white buffalo calf was born.

As the Sun set in the late-summer sky, and as the Moon began to wax full, on August 20, 1994 a white buffalo calf emerged from her mother's womb and drew her first breath alongside the Rock River in Janesville, Wisconsin. Given the name Miracle, the calf soon stirred an immense wave of interest around the world.

Miracle was born into a herd of fourteen buffalo on a forty-six acre family farm owned by David and Valerie Heider. She became the first white buffalo born in more than fifty years. According to the American Bison Association, the odds of a white buffalo calf were one in ten million in the days when buffalo were numerous. Since the buffalo was hunted to near extinction in the late 1800s, they say, the odds of a white buffalo being born have become too high to determine. Yet a white buffalo has been born. In fact, as of Autumn, 2000, seven white buffaloes have come on to the world stage.

Beyond the rarity of the phenomenon, the birth of a white buffalo has significance because of what she represents, as explained in the accounts which have been passed down for generations via the oral tradition. For millions of people the white buffalo calf represents the fulfillment of key Native American understandings.

Legend Has It

Legend has it that long ago the seven council fires of the Lakota Sioux came together in one large camp. There was no game to hunt at that time, and the people were close to starvation. Early one morning the chief, Standing Hollow Horn, sent two young men out to scout for a buffalo herd so that the whole camp might at last set out on a hunt.

According to the book *The Sacred Pipe*, which relates the account of this event given by Black Elk, the scouts roamed the countryside for quite a while. Eventually they encountered a fragrance, a sublime fragrance through which they sensed the imminence of something sacred. Then they saw a holy woman off in the distance. She was dressed in white buckskins and coming toward them across the plains surrounded by a bright light.

One of the scouts found her so beautiful that he could not set aside his desire. He failed to restrain himself, and stepped forward to embrace her. Immediately a fierce dark cloud enshrouded him. When the cloud lifted the hunter had been reduced to a pile of rotting bones, and terrible green snakes were devouring his remains. From this Black Elk drew an eternal truth: "Any man who is attached to the senses and to the things of this world is one who lives in ignorance, and is being consumed by the snakes which represent his own passions."

The other scout knelt to pray as his compatriot perished. The sacred woman spoke, asking him to go back to his people and tell them to prepare. She said that in four days she would visit and bring the people a sacred bundle. The scout did as he was asked. He went back to the camp of the Seven Council Fires, gathered the people in a circle, then told them what had happened, and what the holy woman had asked. The people agreed to welcome the woman, and began to prepare for her.

As she said, on the fourth day the holy woman came to the camp and entered the hoop of the council fires. Some versions of the story say a cloud came down from the sky, and that as the cloud touched the earth a white buffalo calf stepped off, rolled onto the earth, then stood up as a beautiful young woman in a white dress who was carrying a sacred bundle.

According to the telling of Lakota elder Joseph Chasing Horse, as the woman entered into the circle of the nation, she sang a sacred song and carried her bundle into a big lodge that had been prepared for her. There she sat to teach. She spent four days among the people and taught them how to live in the living world. She gave them seven ceremonies, including the *Inipi* (Sweat Lodge), *Hanblechyapi* (Vision Quest), and *Chanupah* (Sacred Pipe). She told them about the meaning of the pipe—how it could represent a respectful joining of the feminine (bowl) and masculine (stem), and how in this way the breath (prayers) could be made visible; and how the pipe could be used to bring peace to warring nations. She told the people also about the sacred value of buffalo, and the many ways the Buffalo Nation acts as a mediator on vast tracts of land, helping to keep the natural balance on Turtle Island (North America). Finally, she taught about the importance of respecting women and children.

When the holy woman was done teaching, she gave the pipe bundle to the people. The Lakota still have the bundle and it is known as the White Buffalo Calf Pipe because it was given by White Buffalo Calf Woman (*Pte San Win*). The pipe is kept by a man who is the 17th generation of his family to hold the pipe for the people. His name is Arvol Looking Horse.

After gifting the people with her teachings and the pipe, White Buffalo Calf Woman departed. As she was leaving the lodge circle toward the setting sun, she turned and told the people that she would return, that she would come when the people needed her, in the dawn of a new day. She told the people to watch for the birth of a white buffalo calf, for that would be a sign that it was near the time when she would return again to help purify the world. She told the people that when she returned she would bring a message of peace, unity and wholeness.

She said she would return in the same manner as she departed. Then as she walked away she rolled over four times, and turned consecutively into a red, a black, a yellow, and finally a white buffalo calf, which walked off into the West. After that day she has been known as Pte San Win (White Buffalo Calf Pipe Woman), and the people have waited for her return.

This aspect of the white buffalo story echoes a perennial theme of return—a mythic archetype. The theme appears in cultures around the world, and is a key part of the stories of many cultural–spiritual heroes, such as Pte San Wi, Viracocha, Quetzalcoatl, the Peacemaker, the Pale One, Christ, Bhudda, Quan Yin, Mohammed, Baha'u'llah, and so forth. All these teachers said they would return to the people in a time of great need.

If all these spiritual heroes are to return at the earth's dark hour to help the people, then one naturally wonders about it. Will they return as individual personalities out and about in the world doing magnificent deeds? Or will they return rather as qualities of spirit that thousands, even millions of people can identify with and express through their lives and actions—as if the virtues of these great spiritual beings lay hidden within each human heart, awaiting the right moment to find expression?

A Father's Sacrifice

Back in 1994 farmer Dave Heider told newspaper reporters that his family felt honored that the white calf had been born at their farm. "It's not something you feel in your head," he said, "it's something you feel in your heart." A Saskatchewan Indian from Canada told him that 500 years ago they saw this coming. He told him they knew the calf would be born to a white man, too. "That's the part that gets me," Heider said.

Ten days after the birth of Miracle, Heider received a phone call from Floyd Looks for Buffalo Hand a Lakota spiritual interpreter from the Pine Ridge Indian Reservation in South Dakota. Mr. Hand, who is also the author of a book entitled *Learning Journey on the Red Road,* told the farmer that the white buffalo calf was safe, protected from evil spirits. But he also said that while Miracle's sire, "Marvin," was all right now, he would soon lay down his life for the white calf.

"When I asked him what he meant," Mr. Heider later explained to reporters, the medicine man told him: "I see a black blockage." The farmer thought little about the message until he walked out to the farmyard to take care of routine chores and found Marvin, the father of the White Buffalo Calf, stretched out on the ground, dead.

Sensing the bull's death, several buffalo cows stood guard at the edge of the pen, as if waiting to pay their last respects. Others charged along the fence line, running back and forth, the earth shaking beneath their hooves. According to news reports at the time, the white buffalo calf never strayed from its mother, but stared with wide eyes at her motionless father.

Not knowing why the six-year-old bull had died, the family called a veterinarian for an autopsy. An hour into the autopsy, Dr. Jim Schwisow called the family over to look at something in one of the bull's stomachs. It was a softball-sized hemorrhage formed near the entrance to the stomach, and deep black in color. Dr. Schwisow eventually discovered two of these black forms, and the cause: several bleeding ulcers in the lower stomach.

One Heart, One Mind, One Spirit

"This is like the Second Coming of Christ on this island of America," Floyd Hand later commented about the birth of Miracle and the teachings of White Buffalo Calf Woman. He said he had his first vision of her in 1968. Then in the Spring of 1994 Hand had another vision. A beautiful lady in a rainbow-colored dress appeared to him in a vivid dream, he said, and told him that she would soon bring a message of peace and unity to the world. "She said she would return when the cherries are black, which happens to be in August," Hand said. And that is just when the first white buffalo calf was born.

Shortly after the birth of the calf, in September, Floyd Hand made a pilgrimage to the Wisconsin family farm with a delegation of Lakota people from the Pine Ridge Reservation in South Dakota. The delegation included Arvol Looking Horse, keeper of the original pipe that was given to the people long ago. Looking Horse had also been one of the four Lakota delegates to the "House of Mica" (Chapter 8) with the Hopi elders for the Cry of the Earth conference.

For 17 generations Looking Horse's family has served as the protector of both the past and the future, Keepers of the Sacred Pipe. Now, with the birth of Miracle, he watched his family's destiny unfold. "The things the elders have talked about for so long, now we can identify with what we have been taught...We are given this time to strengthen each other. This is an important time in history. The prophesies are being fulfilled up to this point. We are starting to see a coming together of people going back to their natural ways," Looking Horse told reporters as he prepared for a welcoming ceremony with the original pipe. He explained that in these times, the white buffalo calf "is like an oasis of divine intervention coming up from Mother Earth."

At the Heider farm, the Lakota delegation welcomed the sacred spirit of White Buffalo Calf Woman. They performed a ceremony with the original pipe given to the people long ago, and they articulated a message of peace. Both Mr. Hand and Mr. Looking Horse spoke at that time of the birth of the white buffalo calf as marking the arrival of a new era of reconciliation among races, and of respect for the Earth.

"We're going to pray for healing of the nations, and we're going to pray for healing of the Earth," Mr. Hand said. "And we're going to be of one heart, one mind, and one spirit, and unify the four sacred colors (races) so that we can stand up for peace. The legend is she (the spirit of the White Buffalo) would return and unify the nations of the four colors—black, red, yellow and white.

"This is an omen that's bringing a new change to a new world," Mr. Hand said. "The 21st century is going to unify all of us. We are here to encourage people to pray for peace. We're going to heal together now." Arvol Looking Horse agreed: "The birth of the white buffalo is an omen of renewed interest in American Indian heritage." He observed that the buffalo's return signifies that "a healing will begin. Dreams and visions will return."

The Four Colors

At that September, 1994 gathering on the Heider farm, Lakota Chief Joseph Chasing Horse—a descendant of Crazy Horse—shared stories and teachings that have been passed on in his family from one generation to the next. He said that soon all humankind will live in harmony with the earth. The first sign of those predictions coming to pass, he said, was the birth of Miracle.

Chasing Horse added that winter counts—which date the telling of the White Buffalo Calf Woman story in sacred ceremonies—confirm that Miracle is the buffalo calf of the prophesy. He said this sign from the Great Spirit—and the ensuing age of harmony and balance it represents—cannot be revoked. "We are praying, many of the medicine people, the spiritual leaders, the elders, are praying for the world. We are praying that mankind does wake up and think about the future, for we haven't just inherited this earth from our ancestors, but we are borrowing it from our unborn children.

"We have been waiting for her return. It is the signal of things to come," he said, adding that the message mankind must heed now is to restore balance and harmony to the earth. "Mother Earth is a living, breathing being who provides all necessities for life. Human beings have been systematically destroying the earth and its ecosystems, which in turn threatens humanity. We live in a time of war, famine and great suffering throughout the world, all because of vengeance, selfishness and greed. Because of these things, our children are suffering.

"We need to teach mankind about harmony, peace, love and understanding," Chasing Horse said. "One day soon all mankind will come together in one circle. We need to learn to tolerate one another's differences. We must take this sign and walk towards that spiritual unity. If we do not turn from the evil ways, destruction will surely follow. That is the message we must heed in order to heal the earth."

Floyd Hand observed that while the white buffalo is part of Native American tradition, it is also significant in the movement to holistic spirituality taking place around the world. "The calf has great healing powers," he explained. "She makes people aware that all living things are equal, not just the Indians, but everyone. The white calf is trying to tell us something. If we listen, there will be peace, love and harmony throughout the earth. That's why so many people have come to Wisconsin to see her." In the years since the birth of Miracle, thousands of people, including many hundreds of First Nations peoples, have flocked to the farm to see the calf.

Over time Miracle has changed the color of her coat in keeping with the colors of the four directions, or four colors of human beings. She was born white, and then over time her coat turned black, then red, then cinnamon yellow. Among native elders it is felt that eventually, down the line, when the races have become unified, she will turn white again.

The idea of the four colors of humanity having dispersed to the four corners of the earth many years ago but being destined eventually to return and unite, is a theme sounded frequently in Native American and other metaphysical teachings. Cherokee and Baha'i spiritual elder Lee Brown shared his view on this theme 1986, in a remarkable talk he gave at the Continental Indigenous Council in Fairbanks, Alaska.

In his talk Mr. Brown said that a long time ago, at the beginning of this cycle of time, Great Spirit gathered the peoples of this earth together on an island which is now beneath the water. At that time He said to the human beings, "I'm going to send you to four directions and over time I'm going to change you to four colors, but I'm going to give you some teachings and you will call these the Original Teachings and when you come back together with each other you will share these so that you can live and have peace on earth, and a great civilization will come about.

"During the cycle of time I'm going to give each of you two stone tablets. When I give you those stone tablets, don't cast those upon the ground. If any of the brothers and sisters of the four directions and the four colors cast their tablets on the ground, not only will human beings have a hard time, but almost the earth itself will die."

"He gave each of us a responsibility and we call that the Guardianship. To the Indian people, the red people, he gave the Guardianship of the earth. We were to learn during this cycle of time the teachings of the earth, the plants that grow from the earth, the foods that you can eat, and the herbs that are healing so that when we came back together with the other brothers and sisters we could share this knowledge with them. Something good was to happen on the earth.

"To the South, he gave the yellow race of people the Guardianship of the wind. They were to learn about the sky and breathing and how to take that within ourselves for spiritual advancement. They were to share that with us at this time.

"To the West He gave the black race of people the Guardianship of the water. They were to learn the teachings of the water, which is the chief of the elements, being the most humble and the most powerful.

"To the North He gave the white race of people the Guardianship of the fire. If you look at the center of many of the things they do you will find the fire. They say a light bulb is the white man's fire. If you look at the center of a car you will find a spark. If you look at the center of the airplane and the train you will find the fire. The fire consumes, and also moves. This is why it was the white brothers and sisters who began to move upon the face of the earth and reunite us as a human family."

All Things Are Sacred

Pipe Keeper Arvol Looking Horse observes that the changes in the color of Miracle's coat coincide with the story of White Buffalo Calf Woman. As remembered by the people, as Pte San Win left the people she rolled over four times, and each time she got up she was a different color. Looking Horse compared the color change to a test of faith. "The way I see things, the calf will eventually turn light again. But we have to become more spiritual. We have to pray. When our spirituality is strong, the calf will become white again."

Looking Horse said it is crucial to focus on the problems of global pollution and disharmony between nations. He said the spirit of the White Buffalo will help unify the different races of humanity, return spirituality and heal the damage caused by pollution. The different colors signify the responsibility of all races to address these issues.

"White Buffalo Calf Pipe Woman taught that each day and all things are sacred, and that we should therefore respect, honor, and commune with all things in the Circle of Life," Looking Horse said. "She spoke of walking in a holy manner. She reminded the people that whatever we do to any other thing or being in the Circle of Life, we do to ourselves—for we are One. Her message was that of a deep sacred ecology. She also reminded the people that without this communion, cooperation, sharing, and unity, we would not be able to move through this old time into a new one."

"Now, as we stand in the midst of immense destruction, brought about by our lack of good relationship with all things, her message is especially important. Miracle appears to remind us to walk in a sacred manner before it is too late."

In the years since the 1994 birth of Miracle, six other white buffalo calves have been born on Turtle Island. As Arvol Looking Horse understands this development from the teachings that have been passed to him, that was expected—at least four white buffalo would be born to mark fulfillment of the prophecy and the imminent return of the spirit of Pte San Win—White Buffalo Calf Woman. In Looking Horse's view that part of the teachings appears to be complete.

White Buffalo Shot

While some aspects of the White Buffalo legend are complete, some other aspects—perhaps deeply karmic aspects—are still being worked out, at least as of the year 2000.

From the beginning of the millennial year great turmoil arose once again, as it has so often in the past, on the Lakota Indian Reservation at Pine Ridge, South Dakota. Protesters occupied the tribal headquarters building in January, 2000 because, they said, tribal affairs and funds had been grossly mismanaged. According to federal statistics, the poverty rate on Pine Ridge at the time of the protest was close to 75%, and had been for years.

The protesters—including Floyd Hand, the same elder who had been gifted with visions concerning the White Buffalo—demanded an end to what they called malfeasance and a vast system of government corruption. They also demanded a return to a traditional style of government, rather than the artificial governmental system imposed by The Indian Allotment Act of 1928 and the Indian Reorganization Act of 1934, which brought the Bureau of Indian Affairs (BIA) into sharp conflict with traditional leaders and elders across Turtle Island. Those laws virtually eliminated time–tested pathways of ascendancy to leadership, and instituted bureaucratic hierarchies. Many observers have long felt the BIA–sanctioned tribal governments are precisely counter to the spirit of Indian culture.

By March of 2000 on the Pine Ridge Reservation, after three prolonged months of acrimony between traditionals and the tribal government, one of the White Buffalo calves was shot and killed under disputed circumstances.

According to the Associated Press (AP) report of the incident, tribal police officials asserted that the buffalo had to be shot because it posed a threat to public safety. The buffalo's owner, Poker Joe Merrival, disputed that. Merrival—a cousin and a close neighbor of Medicine Man Floyd Hand who was at the time still occupying tribal headquarters—said he believed the shooting was unjustified.

The buffalo in question was born as a white calf in May 1996, on Poker Joe's ranch, about a mile north of Pine Ridge village. He named the calf Medicine Wheel. "I had kids pet and feed this buffalo," Merrival told the AP reporter. "It didn't have a mean streak in it." Still, the buffalo was shot.

While the BIA-backed tribal police would not comment on the shooting incident, the police report—supplied by Merrival to the Associated Press—said that the buffalo was shot after an officer found it on a main road one Sunday evening in March, 2000. Officer Alec Morgan wrote in the report that he saw the buffalo in the road, and that two cars narrowly missed the animal. The buffalo was "scared and in a panic," and it charged some vehicles, he claimed.

According to the report, Officer Morgan stopped Leon Poor Bear, who was driving by in a truck. Together, they tried unsuccessfully to chase the buffalo back up the road. The officer said Poor Bear informed him that he had a rifle. "I told Leon to shoot the buffalo for the safety of the community," Morgan stated in his report.

Poker Joe Merrival told reporters that the white buffalo posed no threat to anyone. He said someone must have opened the gate at his ranch to let the buffalo out. He also said that the people chasing the buffalo must have riled it up, because Medicine Wheel was normally calm. "This buffalo was my pet. The white buffalo, I pampered him." Merrival said it made no sense to shoot the buffalo just because it was on the road. "There's horses and cows all over this reservation on the road, but they don't shoot no horses and cows." Still, the white buffalo known as Medicine Wheel was shot by tribal police, and soon died.

"It's still going to be alright," Floyd Hand said in a telephone interview six months after Medicine Wheel—his cousin's buffalo—was killed. He recalled that when he had his vision of White Buffalo Calf Woman in the Spring of 1994, he had been informed that there would soon be many changes. "The government will fall to the side, and the Indian nations will stand up again," he said.

PHOTO 22. *Miracle Moon, a white buffalo, and her calf Rainbow Spirit, also a white buffalo. Rainbow Spirit is the seventh white buffalo calf born since 1994.*
Photo © 2000 by Dena Riley, Dream Maker Bison

The Seventh Buffalo

As if in mythic response to the shooting of the white buffalo on the Pine Ridge Reservation, just a few weeks later, on June 8, 2000, another white buffalo, this one named Miracle Moon, gave birth to yet another white buffalo calf at the Dream Maker Bison Ranch in Colony, Wyoming.

The mother, Miracle Moon, was born three years earlier on April 30, 1997. Before she was one year old she had already turned red, yellow, brown, and then all white. The observed pattern is for her fur to turn colors with the seasons, turning a glowing, silver white in the deepest part of winter.

After Miracle Moon matured, mated, and became pregnant, she gave birth to yet another—the seventh—white buffalo calf. Moments after the birth rancher Jim Riley looked up and saw a rainbow in the sky. Accordingly, Jim and his wife Dena named the new white buffalo calf Rainbow Spirit. Dena says that she and Jim sense that Rainbow Spirit is to be even whiter than her mother, Miracle Moon, and even more extraordinary."

Dena Riley said that Arvol Looking Horse, the keeper of the pipe, visited their ranch on June 22, 2000, just after ceremonies for World Peace Day at nearby Grey Horn Butte. He told the Rileys that Rainbow Spirit was the seventh White Buffalo born so far, and that for the Lakota the number seven signified the end of a cycle. He made no comment on the possibility of an eighth buffalo to mark the start of a new era.

"This is all a little overwhelming for me and my family," Arvol Looking Horse commented in a telephone interview shortly after the birth of Rainbow Spirit. "The mother of this new calf, Miracle Moon, was born three years ago on my birthday, April 30. Now the new white buffalo calf, Rainbow Spirit, was born on June 8—and that's the same date that my father, Stanley Looking Horse, Sr. died on two years ago in 1998. My father was keeper of the pipe before me; he passed it on to me. So these are things my family has taken note of. It makes a deep impression on us."

Whirling Rainbow

Ten months after the birth of Miracle, the first of the white buffalo calves, a coalition of people representing the many colors and spiritual traditions of humanity began walking. On June 23, 1995 they initiated a historic prayer walk from the ancestral territory of the Wampanoag Nation (The People of the Morning Light) along the Atlantic Ocean at First Encounter Beach in the town of Eastham on Cape Cod, Massachusetts. These pilgrims first walked south to Cherokee, North Carolina, then turned to west. Their walk lasted for eight months and spanned 3,700 miles to the shore of the Pacific Ocean at Santa Barbara, California . There it ended with a prayer circle on a windy, cloudy day February 2, 1996.

The epic walk involved approximately forty-five people, and was a response to the call for healing from traditional Native Elders of North America. The vision of the walk took form after the elders spoke at the House of Mica (United Nations headquarters); the vision was reinforced by the birth nine months later of the first White Buffalo. The elders realized that world leaders were not listening, and that the mass media was likewise neglecting their messages. Via the prayer walk, some of the elders hoped to convey the message directly to the people. Yet another goal of the walk was to unite people of all races and religions whose concern for healing the Earth, now and for future generations, far surpassed any racial or religious divisions. The pilgrimage was a gesture of hope and a deed of unity.

Grandfather William Commanda, respected elder of the Algonquin Indian people and keeper of the Seven Fires Wampum belt (Chapter 2), and the principal Algonquin delegate to the "Cry of the Earth" conference at the UN (Chapter 8), was the sponsor for the walk. He joined with other elders and peoples from across the Americas and around the world, who shared a common vision of racial harmony and a world free from environmental destruction.

"The Seven Fires," Grandfather Commanda has often explained, "represent times in the life of the people." The seventh prophet who spoke to the people long ago offered a message of importance to today. "In the time of the Seventh Fire," the prophet said, "new people will emerge. They will retrace their steps to find what was left by the trail long ago. Their steps will take them to the elders, who they will ask to guide them on their journey... If the new people remain strong in their quest, the Sacred Fire will again be lit."

"If people choose the right road, the road of respect and spirituality, then the Seventh Fire will light an Eighth and final Fire, an eternal fire of peace, spirituality, love, brotherhood, and sisterhood."

The pilgrimage—one of many great, long walks taking place in the world—came to be known as the Sunbow 5 Walk for the Earth, and the walkers set out to retrace the footsteps of the ancestors to see what could be found along the site of the trail. According to Tom Dostou and Naoko Haga who shared the vision of the walk, the name of the walk was taken from the Sunbow (also called Sun Dog, or Whirling Rainbow), a natural phenomenon of light in a wide circle around the Sun. On a physical level this wide rainbow circle is said by science to be produced by the reflection of the Sun's light on ice crystals in the sky. Sunbows vary greatly in brightness and distinctness depending on the number and arrangement of the ice crystals in the atmosphere.

Photo 23. *A Sunbow, or Whirling Rainbow, is a natural phenomenon. It appears as a full and wide 360–degree rainbow circle around the sun. In this July,1995 image, a tree shields the sun to reveal the hoop of an early morning Sunbow at Carlson College in Minnesota. (Author photo).*

In some Native communities, the Sunbow or Whirling Rainbow is considered to be a sign from the Creator. Among traditional Hopi, in particular, it been said that a time of great change, or transition on the Earth, would be signaled by an increase in the number of visible Sunbows. This full-circle rainbow around the Sun, some elders say, can be understood as a sign to people of the necessity to live a life in respect and harmony with all the creations that make life possible: plants, animals, waters, minerals, winds, and other human beings.

Jamie Sams, a teacher of Iroquois and Choctaw descent, learned much about the Sunbow when she lived and studied with indigenous elders in Mexico in the1970s. Some of what she learned she later shared in one of her books, *Sacred Path Cards.* "The Whirling Rainbow is the promise of peace among all Nations and people," she wrote. "The Whirling Rainbow will appear in the form of a Sun-Dog to those who are ready to see. The Sun Dog is a full Rainbow Circle around the Sun that has bright white lights at the Four Directions. The Sun-Dog is a rare natural phenomenon that was named by Native Americans. Many Sun-Dogs will be seen around the time of the White Buffalo, which will be the Sky Language sign that the Secret and Sacred Teachings are to be shared with all races. Enough of the Children of the Earth will be awakened to carry the responsibility of the teachings, and the healing process will begin in full swing."

As held in the mythic memory of as many as 200 cultures around the world, at the time of the last great transition from one age to another age, the Earth was purified by a great flood. At that time, it is said, the half-circle of the rainbow was given as a sign of the covenant between the Creator and the people that the world would never again be destroyed by water.

Now in our epoch, when fire is a critical element impacting the world, some traditional peoples see the full circle of the Sunbow, or Sun Dog, as a hopeful sign of another covenant. It is a sign not just of warning, but also of the possibility of peace, respect, and wholeness, just as the Whirling Rainbow is a whole circle. The spiritual ideal is a restoration of the Sacred Hoop, wherein there is fundamental respect of all the parts for one another, and a recognition that together there is a Mystery far greater than the sum of the parts. But these ideals and this pathway must be chosen out of applied intelligence and free will.

The Sunbow walkers encountered many high and low adventures over the course of their pilgrimage. But they did reach the western waters, the Pacific Ocean. On the morning of February 2, 1996, after a pipe ceremony on the beach at Santa Barbara, California, the Seven Fires Wampum Belt was immersed in the Pacific Ocean, and the walkers dispersed to the four directions.

Restoring the Sacred Hoop

At about the time the Sunbow 5 Walk reached the Pacific Ocean in early 1996, Arvol Looking Horse, the Keeper of the Sacred White Buffalo Calf Pipe for the Lakota-Dakota-Nakota Nation, issued a call. He asked all peoples and all nations to declare June 21 as World Peace and Prayer Day each and every year, and encouraged people to journey to the Sacred Places of the Earth to pray on that day.

Looking Horse wrote: "Our prophecies are clear. According to the many respected indigenous spiritual leaders and elders who gathered to 'present signs' from their ancient traditions at the United Nations (Chapter 8), it is time to mend the Sacred Hoop of life on our Earth Mother. The birth of the White Buffalo Calf (August 20, 1994) let us know that we are at a crossroads: we either return to balance or face global disaster. It is our duty to journey to the sacred places of the world and pray for world peace. If we do not do this our children will suffer."

"According to our Star Knowledge, there are six stars which designate six sacred sites within the Black Hills of South Dakota (*Pa Ha Sapa*). These are sacred places to pray. We are told that there are similar sacred sites every hundred miles around Mother Earth. One of those places—the place where Looking Horse and many hundreds of other people went for the first World Peace Day on June 21, 1996—was Grey Horn Butte in the Black Hills of Wyoming. It was near Grey Horn Butte that Pte San Wi made her first appearance, bringing the gift of the Sacred White Buffalo Calf Pipe 19 generations ago, the same Pipe that Chief Looking Horse cares for.

Grey Horn Butte was renamed "Devil's Tower" many decades ago, when missionaries sought to stigmatize the Native prayer rituals at this site. Devil's Tower became briefly famous in the 1980s when depicted as the site of UFO landings in the popular film, *Close Encounters of the Third Kind.*

"There are sacred places like this all over the Earth," Looking Horse wrote in his call to prayer. These sacred places are, for the body of our Mother Earth, similar to what people in Eastern spiritual traditions understand as the chakras (wheels of spiritual energy) on our human bodies. They are sensitive openings essential for health. On the planet sacred sites serve as gateways, or connections to Mother Earth. Praying and meditating at such sites is said to be a key in bringing about global healing for Mother Earth and her children.

"We ask all people of all faiths to journey to these many Sacred Places around the world each year on June 21," Looking Horse requested, "and to pray with us according to the traditions of their hearts. We ask all peoples to organize their ceremonies at their sacred sites so they will be praying at the same time as we are.

"The vision is for all continents, no matter what belief in the Creator, to pray and meditate with one another, to obtain an energy shift to heal the ozone layer and achieve a consciousness toward attaining peace, the main key. The ozone layer is now realized as Mother Earth's Spiritual embodiment, what can be understood as her aura," Looking Horse said. "Damage to the ozone layer is creating global warming and must be healed for the next Seventh Generation to survive."

Chapter Ten

Tales of Alinta:
Rainbow Down Under

From her home in Australia, Lorraine Mafi-Williams has journeyed around the world, including several pilgrimages to Turtle Island. Known also as Alinta—Woman of the Fire—Lorraine relates the Aboriginal stories that are the heritage of Australia, the Land of the Everlasting Spirit. She also tells stories of the ancient linkages between Australia and America, a linkage that she says will play a critical part in the reemergence of the rainbow.

Lorraine says a central part of her life mission is to help reestablish the legendary and critical link between the Aborigines of Australia and the American Indians of Turtle Island. She tells her tales with strong, expressive eyes, captivating turns of language, and film.

"I was born beside a fresh water spring on the outskirts of Purfleet Mission at Taree," Lorraine explains. "It was on the eighth of August, 1940, at dawn. They tell me I was the last baby to be born in the traditional way. My mother was accompanied by her aunt and the midwife. That day, a white crane came to feed in the water nearby. The old women said this was a good omen.

"My mother was a traditional medicine woman and healer, and my father was a linguist. His job was to teach and pass on the many dialects

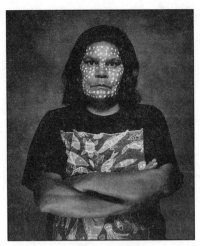

PHOTO 24. *Alinta (Lorraine Mafi–Williams) Photo by Matthew Tung.*

associated with the north coast tribes of New South Wales. He was also an initiated man, having learned the rules and lore of his tribe, the Bundjalung of Lismore. My mother was a Thungutti woman, whose ancestors originated west of the Blue Mountains."

As a child, Lorraine was a victim of the "stolen generation" of Aborigine children the government ordered removed from the care of their parents and put to work in white households. Pressed into domestic service, Lorraine did not see her parents from age twelve until nearly her twentieth birthday. Then her education in the rich tradition of the Aborigine people began in earnest. "I was taken back to the Dreamtime teachings by the old people, beginning with the Githrabaul tribe, where I met and eventually married a Githrabaul man. Starting with my father-in-law and his mother, I was told many things of a deep cultural and spiritual nature, and I was initiated in these teachings. The Dreamtime is the source of both past reality and future possibilities."

Throughout her adult life, Lorraine has also been trained by Mrs. Millie Boyd. Known widely as Aunt Millie, she is an elder of the Githrabaul people, a clan of the Bundjalung tribe, whose ancestral territory is along the North coast of New South Wales. Aunt Millie is a "clever woman"—a shaman and medicine woman trained in the old ways of the Aborigines. She is the traditional custodian of Mount Warning (Wollombin) and also of Nimbin Rocks, Tooloom Falls, and Crown Mountain.

Wollombin is a sacred mountain, the first place that the sun touches in Australia each morning. Aboriginal people believe that the mountain absorbs the rays of the sun, which activate a large rose-quartz crystal hidden in its depths. In turn, the crystal is said to send the rays to Ayers rock, or Uluru, which then transmits these rays to Tibet.

Just as Native Americans have ancient and profound ties to the people of Tibet, so do the Aborigines. All three are linked: the Tibetans, the Native Americans, and the Australian Aborigines.

Lorraine says that according to an ancient Tibetan Buddhist prophecy, the Aborigines and Tibetans would come together again when the balance of the world was threatened by greed, when it was time to make the transition to a New Age. The prophecy stated that an era would come when the sacred teachings would be suppressed inside Tibet, as has happened since China invaded that small nation in the late 1950s. The Tibetans would then reappear in a southern land with a great red rock at its center. Since the early 1980s Tibetan Lamas, including Lama Zazep Tulku, have been making pilgrimages to the massive red rock at the heart of Australia: Ayer's Rock, or Uluru, as it was named in the original language. There they join in prayers and ceremony with other keepers of the Earth.

Aunt Millie, who had attained the age of ninety-six in 1991 but, who has since died, was especially privy to this three-part relationship, for she was the keeper of Wollombin, the sacred mountain believed to be the home of the Native American spirit Waugatha. Some years ago Aunt Millie delegated Lorraine as her "liaison officer" to the outside world. In a show of Aboriginal protocol, Aunt Millie never talks directly of the most sensitive spiritual matters. She talks to Lorraine, and Lorraine passes on the information.

Lorraine's teachings encompass all of the traditional Aboriginal lore. Her tribal name, Alinta, or Woman of the Fire, was given to her because she has been trained in what she calls fire medicine. She now has three married sons and nine grandchildren. She has traveled much of the world, and she holds the distinction of being the first Aboriginal filmmaker in Australia

"Along the many paths I have been drawn to over the course of my life have been politics, community development, health, housing, and education. However, it was in the arts that I excelled and found the most enjoyment. From writing I advanced into film making," she relates.

Lorraine began her film career in 1973, when Aunt Millie asked her to make a film about some of the sacred sites of Australia that are being threatened by mining and development. "I wanted to fulfill Aunt Millie's request," Lorraine says, "and it all just came together, neat as you please." Over the years Lorraine has worked as an advisor and assistant on many critically acclaimed Australian films: *Journey Among Women, The Last Wave, Chant of Jimmy Blacksmith, Women of the Sun,* and *Cyclone Tracey.* She has won awards for producing and directing two films: *Sacred Ground,* and *Eelemarni.*

A central focus of Lorraine's current work is using her skills as a storyteller and a filmmaker to call attention to the plight of the Earth's protective energy grid through a film called *The Sickness Country.* The film will tell of the imminent threat posed by the mining of minerals from Coronation Hill, the head of the Rainbow Serpent.

Land of the Everlasting Spirit

"We, the Australian Aboriginals, have been on our traditional land, the Land of the Everlasting Spirit, for tens of thousands of years," Lorraine explains. "Our culture is rivaled by no other, though we have been in seclusion for the last two hundred years. We are emerging from that seclusion now to show ourselves as no one has ever seen us. Our creation stories take us back into the Dreamtime, beginning when the Earth was one land mass [Scientists place this phase of the Earth's development 250 to 300 million years ago, and they refer to the single land mass as Pangaea]. At that time, the four races—red, yellow, black, and white—lived side by side. There we lived as one people, creating a world of harmony, balance, and mystery.

"As Aboriginals we have kept our culture intact for thousands of years, into the present time. Now we are becoming ready to share our wondrous culture with the other people of the world. That is my work through my teaching and my films.

"What a lot of people tend to forget is that my country has only been occupied for two hundred years by the British. It only took white people fifty years to destroy a million years of our culture, but the core of it still remains strong. We haven't forgotten. Our elders are telling us to go out and tell everyone so that no one can say they didn't hear."

"Whenever our elders, or shaman people—all our elders are shaman people—talk about our history and our beginning, our creation, they always talk about the time when the Earth was one land mass. They speak of the time before the cataclysm came that split the Earth up into the continents.

"This is our story, our mythology. Our land, Australia, is called *Arunta*, the Land of the Everlasting Spirit. Our old people told us that we had come from a planet that had seen its time and just blew up.

"See, our people were like refugees, and they went and lived in the stars in the Milky Way. Then seven spirit brothers and seven spirit sisters came to Earth. They came when the Earth was one big landmass.

"They came to erect an energy grid. Because, you see, the planet Earth is among the smallest of planets. And it is really not in the galactic system where all the other planets exist. We believe Earth is just a little bit outside the plane of the Milky Way galaxy in space. Because the Earth is so small, when the planets line up in a certain way the pull of galactic energy is so strong that it could just suck planet Earth into the spiral plane of the galactic system and toss it all around.

"So, my people were given the knowledge to create this energy grid because the planet that they were previously on did not have such a protective structure and it was destroyed. They realized that their new home, the Earth, needed to have such an energy grid in strong and healthy condition to withstand the periodic energy pulsations from the galaxy. Otherwise, it would quickly be drawn into the plane of the galaxy and experience devastating turbulence.

"But my ancestors had learned this lesson, and so they came to Earth to erect an energy grid, or an Earth truss, to help the Earth when it undergoes its changes. My ancestors' responsibility, and my people's responsibility still, is to the energy grid."

Sacred Rainbow Serpent

The protective system that Lorraine refers to as an energy grid is a system of energy lines in and around the entire planet. As a system, it is similar to the meridians of energy in the human body that are used by practitioners of acupuncture. "In our old way," Lorraine says, "we call the energy grid Boamie, the sacred Rainbow Serpent, whose colors reflect the beauty of the Earth and sky, the rainbow. The multicolored coils of the Rainbow Serpent are reflected in the precious stones that are concealed in the Earth's crust.

"It's called the Rainbow Serpent because it's got all the colors of the rainbow: the gold and silver, of course, and the diamonds, the rubies, the emeralds, and the uranium. You see, it's the foundation, the Earth's crust. They are the particular substances that keep the energy grid strong and the Earth solid when the planets line up every so often and threaten to draw the Earth into the galactic energy swirl.

"Since my people erected the energy grid, the Earth just sort of sails through the periodic planetary lineups without any difficulties. So that's my people's responsibility. Both men and women are very knowledgeable in how the energy grid works, the whole system. We know what each mineral in the Earth is supposed to do, and what men's and women's responsibilities are to keep the grid strong and healthy."

"We are very concerned about the energy grids of the Earth," Lorraine says. "They are there to help the Earth maintain balance. Crystals and other minerals feed energy to the energy grid. They have been used for millions of years that way. For the health of the Earth, the crystals must be free to let energy flow to the grid.

"But now minerals, metals, and jewels have been removed from the Earth to such an extent that the balance is in jeopardy. Uranium, in particular, is important for this task. When it is all gone, the Earth will be right out of balance."

Since the advent of nuclear power in the 1930s and 1940s, extensive mining projects have burrowed into sources of uranium in many sensitive sites around the world. These areas include the ancestral land of the Hopi Indians in the U.S. Southwest, the high Himalayas long guarded by the Tibetan lamas, and the sacred lands of the Australian Aborigines. All of these key spiritual areas—Tibet, Hopiland, and key sites in Australia—remain under assault for their mineral (material) assets, and largely neglected for their spiritual assets. For example, Kakadu National Park in the Northern Territories, is one of Australia's famed beauty spots, and it attracts thousands of visitors every year. It also forms part of the traditional land of the Jawoyn people, who, like all Aboriginal peoples, trace their ancestry back some forty thousand years. These days, the Jawoyn refer sorrowfully to their land as "the sickness country"— hence, the name of one of Lorraine's films.

On paper, at least, Kakadu is territory belonging to the British Crown, which can lease it out to Australian and foreign interests. There is intense interest in the area, for it is rich in platinum, palladium, and uranium.

Lorraine says all of these coveted substances are critical components of the Rainbow Serpent, the protective energy grid. In fact, according to the Aborigines, this site is the most sacred and critical in Australia. The British coincidentally named it Coronation Hill, but for many thousands of years the Aborigines have known it as the crown, or head, of Boamie, the Rainbow Serpent.

According to the elders of the Jawoyn people, Coronation Hill is part of an extremely powerful dreaming, that, if disturbed, will cause sickness, fires, earthquakes, and volcanic eruptions that will obliterate wide areas of the Earth. For years, the Jowyn people have been struggling to keep mining interests away from Coronation Hill. Two uranium mines have already been opened. Since there is much money to be made, development threats continue to arise.

The Jowyn people had hoped that by compromising with tourism, for which they receive no monetary gain, they could soften any governmental hard-line attitude on mining. But the requirements of the modern material world are routinely in sharp conflict with the spiritual vision of Earth-based peoples. The issue at stake, as ever, is the concept of land ownership.

Even beyond land ownership and the long-lived and deadly poisonous effects of nuclear waste, Lorraine believes there are other crucial considerations in this matter: "This mining has an influence on the human race, too, and the human body. The human being is a link between the heavens and the Earth. By keeping our bodies in balance and harmony, we can keep the Earth healthy, and that in turn supports our health. You see, it's a cycle. I use crystals in healing, but I do not believe they should be taken from the Earth to be used as ornaments. It's more valuable to leave them in the Earth. The same with the uranium."

Crucial Juncture

Based on her traditional training and her meetings with other Aboriginal elders, Lorraine says we are again at a crucial juncture of the Earth's development. "We have been told that within every one million years, there is a 7,000-year-long Earth shift. Then we begin to go into a new world, like we are doing now. By our reckoning, we are actually at the end of a 7,000-year shift now, and beginning to enter a new million-year long epoch.

"Our people and our teachings are very similar to the teachings of the North American Indian people. But we have different interpretations, and we know our responsibility: taking care of the Earth through the energy grids. It's very similar to what the Native Americans teach about. We do that by giving thanks to the Earth through songs, dances, and ceremonies.

"Right now there's two things. The Earth is undergoing its Earth changes, which is normal for this time in our development. But because there's been so much destruction to the energy grid, especially the gold, which is nearly exhausted already—and now they are after the uranium—there is great danger to the stability of the Earth.

"Gold has driven men mad for thousands of years, leading them to lie, steal, cheat, murder, and make war—all this wickedness to get the gold. Humanity has become greedy and, as a result, wicked. That has led to fighting, war, and disease. People have forgotten their responsibility to the Earth for want of the gold. Now it's the uranium.

"As a consequence of all this mining, there's not enough of the Rainbow Serpent left to help the Earth undergo its seven-thousand-year shift in a safe way. It's all topsy-turvy. Without the balance of the minerals and a healthy energy grid, we cannot pass through the current planetary alignments, and we may be drawn into the plane of the galaxy."

"As well as the Earth, humanity has to go through its changes. We've all got to rejuvenate and to create a new world on this same physical substance. And we are going through it. There's no safe place on Earth. We've just got to ride it out. But if we are in balance within ourselves, and in balance with the Earth, then we are healthy.

"At the end of each change—every time we come into a new world—the Great Creator says 'OK, humanity, you must start your change now, too, and go into the new world. But you must do it in accordance with the Earth, as well as yourself, with heart.'"

Wollombin

With a steely look of certainty, Lorraine that says one of the secrets that needs to be revealed now is the story of Wollombin, or Mount Warning, and the spirit of Waugatha, who is said to inhabit this sacred mountain.

"If you go back to the time when the Earth split up from one land mass into the continents, it was another time of Earth changes. Humanity was wicked in those days, too. Even your own books in Western civilization speak of Noah and the ark and how there was wickedness on the Earth.

"The Native American people say they rode the changes out on the back of a turtle—a land mass like a turtle, Turtle Island. My people rode the flood out by climbing upon a big red rock called Uluru—now usually called Ayer's Rock. Uluru simply means 'the big rock.' Uluru is seven miles around and one mile up.

"Our people teach that when the Earth was one big land mass, Wollombin was one of four big mountains that housed huge crystals. They are the activators for the crystal grid and for the energy grid that protects the Earth. Perhaps the Himalayas might have one, and perhaps the Andes in South America might have one. I don't know for sure, but I know Wollombin is one, the one in the East. We are east of the rest of the world in our tradition, but I don't know what the other mountains are.

"When the Earth split, people were running in confusion, and some of my people stayed on other continents—though they are all extinct now. Some other nationalities stayed Down Under, but now they are extinct, too. But as our old people recall, when the people ran, a White Buffalo ran with them in Australia."

As recorded voluminously in the lore of the Lakotas, the Crow, the Chippewa, and other Native American tribes, the White Buffalo is one of their most sacred symbols. It represents purity, as well as sacrifice for the benefit of all the people. The White Buffalo is regarded as a sign that prayers are being heard and that the promises of prophecy are being fulfilled.

According to Aboriginal legend, at the time the Earth broke up and a White Buffalo ran with the people, a sacred mountain that was under the care of the North American Indian people also broke off and came with them. Instead of remaining with the North American continent of the Red Race, it stayed on the east coast of what is known today as Australia, the Land of the Everlasting Spirit.

"That mountain is Wollombin, or Mount Warning," Lorraine says. "And it is the mountain of which Aunt Millie Boyd is custodian. See, the story of that mountain has been handed down for thousands of years, through the generations. At the time that mountain split off with the Australian continent, there was a very high, powerful shaman or medicine man of the Indian people who stayed on that mountain. Wollombin, you see, means 'eagle.' The spirit is still there, and his name is Waugatha.

"That mountain is in my aunt's country. She's the last custodian of it, though, now that it has been handed back into the care of the North American Indian people. You see, I came here to America in 1988 to look and see if there was any memory among the Indian people of their lost mountain. And there was someone here, a medicine man, who remembered. I found him. Ever since, there have been Indian people who have come to visit the mountain and who have met with Aunt Millie to hear about and learn about Wollombin and Waugatha. See, there's the connection between Australia and North America—between the Aborigines and the Native Americans. It has something to do with the Native American relationship to the Sun and the Sun Dance."

Aboriginal Persecution

"Prior to 1975," Lorraine relates, "we were governed by the government. A group of white people set themselves up as the governing body over the Aboriginals in 1816, and they called themselves the Aboriginal Protection Board. Now, they started out with very good intentions, because at that time there were a lot of massacres going on with my people. We were being slaughtered by the settlers, and practically wiped out. So this governing agency formed themselves into a board, and to protect us they placed us on missions, which are much the same thing as the Indian reservations in America.

"Where missions and reservations are concerned, it's exactly the same with the North American Indian people and my people, the Aboriginal people. The Aboriginal Protection Board was finally abolished in 1967. But prior to that the board had become very oppressive. The rules were that Aboriginals could not own land, could not own money or receive money, and could not be educated. Aboriginal children were removed from their parents, placed in institutions, and trained as domestics and laborers—a slave class, based on the Negro race system in America. You see, the British came here to America, but they sent their convicts to my country. We got the worst of the worst.

"Aborigines in Australia have suffered under terrible persecution since England established its penal colonies there two hundred years ago. Over the years, the Aborigines have been attacked, herded onto reserves, and discriminated and legislated against. In many instances they have been forced into slavery. They are still engaged in an ongoing struggle for land rights—rights they say are essential for the well being of the world.

"We were freed in 1967 after a referendum," Lorraine says. "We were freed from the missions. We can go anywhere now, but before that we needed permission—a twenty-four-hour citizen's pass to go anywhere, to move. Even though life was terrible on the missions, they allowed our people to keep the language, the traditions, the culture, the law, everything going—despite all the pressures.

"We adopted some of the Christianity that was pressed upon us. We went to church and Sunday school. We listened to the doctrine, but we never accepted it, because we only have one God, one Creator, and nobody in between. I could be corrected here, but, as I understand it, Australian Aboriginal people and Native American Indian people did not follow Christian teachings by and large, nor did they follow a leader like Jesus, Buddha, or Mohammed. We never did worship a human being. We stuck to one God in heaven and one Mother Earth. And we carried out our responsibility to the animals, the birds, the fish, and to Mother Earth. As far as I know."

A Council of Elders
"Our elders met in 1975 in the capital city, Canberra, and drew together over 350 of the Aboriginal people," Lorraine recounts. "At that time they gave out their predictions of the changes that are happening and coming. It was a closed meeting just with us Aboriginal people. What they said is exactly what the Native American people are saying. When the Earth undergoes its last Earth shift—very soon—some of the land-mass will go under, just as in ancient times Atlantis went under the water. At the same time, other landmasses will rise, which will bring the continents back closer. Australia will be east, then, of America.

"Back in 1975, the elders, seven of them, sat in a circle in the center. The spokesman stood up and looked at us and said, 'Which way are we going to go in the future?' And then he threw into the center of the circle first a *Bible*, and then a little bark painting—which is the way our people have recorded things since ancient times. I thought, 'gee, he's asking us to make a choice between religion and our culture.' But that wasn't it. Their philosophy was that the *Bible* and our teachings are the same as God's law. I didn't understand that for nearly fifteen years. But now I know. I realize and understand what the old people were saying.

"I resisted at first and thought, 'no way am I going to try and teach white people all this about Wollombin and Waugatha, the energy grid and all the rest. Wouldn't I be selling out, or be betraying my ancestral heritage?'

"But back in 1975, the elders said 'You will know when the time comes, what decision to make.' And whatever it was, it would be fine by them because each and every white person must know our story and our teachings before we go into the new world. Despite all that's happened to our people, our elders said that we must teach the white people our culture. We've got to all go into the new world as one people. We were told to go out and start teaching because, as our elders put it, not one white person should turn around and say to us, 'We were not told. We were not warned.'

"At that very same meeting, our elders said that once all humanity settles down into the Earth changes, then industry goes, commerce goes, money goes, governing bodies go. North American Indian people and Aboriginal people will be among the leaders in power, in politics, in government—but not the way it is now. They said we would go back to a cultural beginning, to meeting again in a circle, in the Sacred Hoop. It was all mind blowing to us then, in 1975, but it has made more and more sense as time has gone on."

The Predictions

As she meets with groups in America and around the world, Lorraine shares some of the predictions that were voiced at the Canberra meeting of the Aborigines: "As of 1975, our old people started to tell us of the changes that would come about in our country. They spoke of the great droughts that would come, and the breakdown in the energy grid. The elders spoke of all the trends of the Great Purification that the Hopi Indian people and others talk about.

"So far, many of the major things that they mentioned have come to pass. The greatest and most important thing they said was that our young men would shed their blood for our land, but not in a warlike way. We Aboriginal people have never been warlike. We have just continued to support the energy grid, and we have made a deliberate decision not to involve ourselves in hierarchies or power struggles or establishing an army. It was always peace, equality, companionship, and love—all based specifically on love, the great emotional binder. We stuck to God's laws, like the Ten Commandments. The First Commandment is universal: Thou shalt not kill. There's no exceptions. We've always obeyed that law.

"What's happening in Australia is that the Ku Klux Klan is very strong. They use that name Down Under, too. The Klan has established itself very strongly in my country, and you know what their philosophy is: hate and all that sort of stuff. There are many groups and committees whose aim is to keep Australia white. Now, how they got that idea, when we were there so long before them, I will never understand.

"Anyway, they out and out began to go after us and the Vietnamese boat people. The Klan operates out of every prison in Australia. In recent years there have been over 260 deaths of our young people, deaths in custody. That aspect is very damaging to our people. And now the Klan is showing themselves elsewhere, especially in the outback, in the little towns.

"That's all part of the prophecy of our old people. With the Ku Klux Klan, of course, comes the occult, black medicine, black magic, and all that sort of stuff. That also is part of the prophecy, because evil, too, has got to make itself or break itself.

"Part of the prophecy from our people is that it will be the children of the world that will suffer at the hands of evil. If you look at it from a world perspective, and take Chernobyl, you'll begin to see. Our old people predicted Chernobyl in 1975, and now it's the children of Chernobyl that are suffering. Thousands of them are coming down with leukemia in Russia and Europe. I don't care if the Russians or whoever say they're responsible, it's Australia that's ultimately responsible for Chernobyl because the uranium comes from there, from our land. It should never have been dug up.

"When our old people said the world would suffer, the children would suffer, they looked at it that way, because they started from home. So, the children of the world are suffering. They are seeds of the new world. Likewise, you've probably heard of the plight of the Romanian children, and in America there is so much child abuse. It's all over the world. That's what our old people were talking about in 1975."

Come to Wollombin

According to Lorraine, each Aboriginal tribe has a responsibility. In a tribe, one person looks after the environment, and one caretakes the animals, and one looks after the fish of the sea, and so on for all the other dimensions of life and creation. "The last person who was caretaker in my father's tribe, the Bundjalung, was my father's niece, whose name was Mary Wilson. We called her Sister Mary and she passed away in 1991. She was the last custodian for the dolphins.

"Two years before Harmonic Convergence in 1987, Sister Mary was told by the dolphins that something very big was going to happen related to the Earth changes. They didn't tell her what it was. But my Aunt Millie was also told to prepare Wollombin for a big happening related to Earth changes.

"Aunt Millie told me, in 1986, to look for a Thunder Rock, a Thunder Egg, and to place it in the East, at the base of Wollombin (Mount Warning). So we did that. I found the rock, which was a geode about the size of a loaf of bread, and we placed it at the base of Wollombin in the East.

"I work in education sometimes, so I was invited to an education conference in New Zealand. It was at a big center, and I was looking at all the fliers tacked to the wall, and one caught my eye. The words seemed strange to me, and they still seem strange, for it talked about Harmonic Convergence and Quetzalcoatl, the Rainbow Feathered Serpent of the Americas. Then I got a message from Spirit that this was the big happening that we were being told to prepare Wollombin for.

"I copied the flier and took it back to Aunt Millie and spread the word to come to Wollombin at Harmonic Convergence. Among the New Age people in Australia, the message went out that Uluru was the focal point, and that's where everyone should gather. But we knew that

Wollombin was the place. All these esoteric people jumped on the bandwagon and sent everyone to Uluru. But we just said no."

Waiting Through the Night

"We got it all organized," Lorraine says. "We encouraged as many people as possible to go to Wollombin for Harmonic Convergence. That was part of what the old people were talking about in 1975. We got over six hundred people there, and we stayed opposite the mountain. We didn't stay where all the people were camping. There were too many people; we wouldn't have been able to breathe, let alone talk. So a group of us Aboriginal people sat all night on the other side of the mountain the night before Harmonic Convergence. We were told something was going to happen on the mountain, so we waited.

"About quarter past two or half past two in the morning, we noticed that it was getting bright. You see, the mountain looks over the ocean, and we were slightly inland. As it started to get bright, I looked at Aunt Millie, because it was not time for the moon to rise. There was only half a Moon then, not much, but it was pretty bright. As we watched, we saw, at first, a fire like the sun rising. It was as bright as if the Sun was coming up.

"What happened in a split second was that the moon and the sun moved. The moon started to set—and the sun started to rise, even at this early hour. They came—bang—together, then dropped. We thought that was something, that's OK, it came to pass. Then we saw a silver beam coming out of the mountain, and the silver beam changed into Waugatha, the Native American spirit who resides on the mountain. Then it gradually slithered into the snake, and Waugatha changed to the human, and then, all of a sudden, Wollombin and the eagle as one. It all came together as one on the top—the silver beam, the Rainbow Feathered Serpent, Quetzalcoatl, and Waugatha.

"For us, this was a confirmation that the mountain belongs to the Red Race. Aunt Millie then said it was time to tell everyone the story of Wollombin and Waugatha and who really owns that mountain. It's also when Aunt Millie decided that the care of the mountain should be handed back to the Red Race.

"When I started being trained as a healer, one of my teachers said I would travel the world to share and teach and learn. Auntie Millie said to be sure and tell the North American people about this mountain, and that the responsibility for caring for it was no longer ours. This I have done, everywhere I have traveled. I've met many Indian people, and I've told them."

The New World Has Started

As Lorraine sees it, Harmonic Convergence signaled the end of the old world. "The Earth is starting its repairs. It needed human help on August 16 and 17, 1987, because the only mineral that hasn't been taken too much is, thank goodness, the crystal.

"Elders from all points on the Earth began to meet at sacred sites on their own land in 1988 to make prayers and ceremonies. The ancient people are seeing that now they have to come together and make world decisions. We have to go back to our Dreamtime culture before we can come forward. All the tribal elders from around the world are beginning to come together and to meet as one big committee of elders to determine the cultural beginning of the new world, the New Age.

"The new world has started. Teaching, politics, and education are eventually going to be based on the laws and politics of this international committee of elders."

Lorraine feels the people of the world can help the transition to the new time by helping to prevent the mining of the Rainbow Serpent—helping to ensure that there will be no more unconscious mining of uranium and other precious materials. The Australian government has promised the Aborigines that it will not mine. But whenever there is an economic slump, they think the only way out of that slump is to exploit the Earth—to mine the uranium at sites like Coronation Hill, the crown of the Rainbow Serpent. "That's the pressure that's being put on our people," Lorraine says, "and on all the people of Australia.

"When we say we want land rights, what we really want is the right to protect that land—not so much for our own gain, because materialism is not part of our culture. We didn't care when we weren't allowed money. Money was insignificant to us. If we got it, poof, it was gone: we spread it around among all the people. We tried to go into these national parks and explain about the sacred sites and the energy grid, and to say that because of this they were dangerous sites to dig into the Earth. But they don't listen.

"Harmonic Convergence brought the world's attention to the necessity of energizing the Earth's energy grid and of reconstructing the intricate systems protecting the balance of the Earth—Grandmother Spider's web system, to use the Native American way of speaking about this."

There are other ways modern people can help restore the health of the web, or energy grid, so that we may pass through this time of transition in better order, Lorraine says. "First," she says, "go to the elders. Listen to what the elders say. Here in America and around the world, listen to the elders. And then make prayers and ceremonies for the Earth. Take action. Plant trees and flowers. Good diet, proper exercise, and prayer can also help us to stabilize our lives so that we may offer them in service toward stabilizing life on Earth."

What Alinta Was Shown
In 1984, Lorraine was gifted with a powerful vision. "What I was shown," she says, "was a vision similar to visions I have heard many Native Americans speak about. I was shown this outer circle representing the women, and the next circle in represents the men. Then there's a little circle in the center, which is the children. Now this is symbolic of what the new world is going to look like. It's going to be a beautiful golden world.

"Most people will be in the four golden rays of this circle. But those who are still trying to sort themselves out and find the meaning of their lives will be in between the golden rays, waiting. These areas are all in motion. The rays in between the golden rays are purple rays or violet rays. The people who are in the violet rays have the opportunity to push through and step into the golden rays when they make their minds up. That's because this golden world has to be pure. So this lot in the violet rays are give the opportunity to choose. This violet ray has got to be cleared. That's what we believe. It'll happen that fast. The elders feel that we will pass through this time of transition OK, even if they mine uranium at Coronation Hill, the head of the Rainbow Serpent.

"This is part of the purification. In the back of the *Bible*, the book of Revelation talks about the Heavenly Host. Now the Heavenly Host, as our elders explain them to us, are our planetary helpers, who

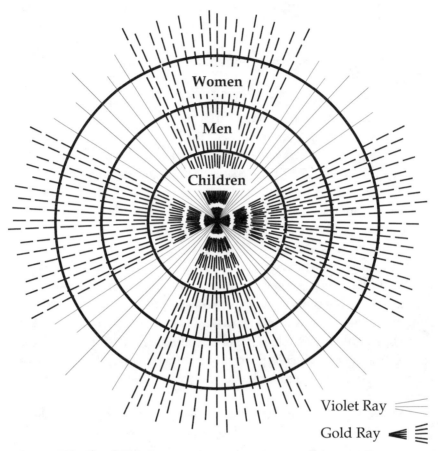

FIGURE 10. Alinta's Vision

get their direction from the Creator, God. God told our planetary helpers, the Heavenly Host, only to monitor and support the Earth. They do not interfere with humanity. We have spirit helpers, too. They are our ancestors' spirits or the spirits of anybody who is not living in a body now. Spirit helpers are the ones who look after humanity. You see, our Heavenly Host does not interfere with the spiritual development and destiny of humanity. They only monitor the Earth and Earth movements.

"The Native Americans refer to the Great Mystery, but our people always refer to God as the Beloved One. The Beloved One said to the Heavenly Host, 'I will not let my Earth be destroyed.' So God asked the

Heavenly Host only to monitor the Earth and see that it gets safely through.

"So there may be volcanoes and earthquakes and storms and diseases and the hate groups, but we get through it all because the Spirit will illuminate the wars, the Ku Klux Klan, the diseases, and all that. Some will perish; they'll go altogether; they'll die. But some will live. There's a real demand that we wake up and listen closely and follow our hearts and spirits.

"Right now there are four areas of gold and four areas of the violet ray. But that will all close in a circle when it's ready. That will all become one pure golden world, one circle, the Sacred Hoop.

"Each indigenous race will have its own system, its own interpretations or teachings, its own way. The Earth will be guided by a council of eight elders, one woman and one man from each of the four races. That's the Aboriginal way of seeing things.

"In the new world, the form of communication will be with computers, TVs, and so forth. People will use the technology that is the gift of the light-skinned race to communicate with each other and with Spirit. The gifts of all the races will be honored and used, too. This is the rainbow of humanity. This is what our old people say."

As It Was in the Beginning

Despite all the upheaval of the Earth changes, Lorraine is filled with hope. She says that watching the rainbows, and supporting them with prayer and stewardship of the Earth, are two things that anyone can do in these troubled times. "The rainbow is a form of illumination for humanity. One of the signs our elders looked for in ancient times was a perfect rainbow, a perfect one. They do ceremonies periodically to keep the energy grid healthy. They would use the rainbows to monitor what they had done. If they did the ceremonies right and the energy grid was healthy, then the rainbows would be perfect. Some of our old people could summon up the rainbow the way some Native American medicine people could bring rain. My father was one that could bring rain. Others could bring the rainbow with their prayers.

"As soon as the rainbow appeared, our elders would look at it closely, carefully, for little flaws. Were all the colors as bright as they should be? Did the rainbow arc from one place on the Earth to another, or was it incomplete? They'd size it up carefully. That way they could see if Boamie, the Rainbow Serpent, needed something—if it was damaged or incomplete in some way. They could tell that by studying the rainbow in the sky for imperfections. The rainbow in the sky is a reflection of the Rainbow Serpent of the Earth; it reflects the health of the Earth and its energy grid."

Lorraine says this may be the reason that when we see rainbows in the modern world, they are so often dull or distorted. Or, they do not reach completely from one point on the Earth to another point; only one end of the rainbow touches the ground. The rainbow is a reflection of the health of the Earth underneath it, and in many places the Earth is sick now.

"Whenever our old people were traveling, or were out and about," Lorraine says, "they'd call up the rainbow and check the energy grid. That was their responsibility. It was an ongoing thing, and it's ongoing today."

"The rainbows will be perfect again as soon as the Sacred Hoop closes, as soon as the golden circle of the new world is complete. It will be perfect. The Earth will already have undergone its changes and all that sort of thing. It will be rejuvenating, new life. The rainbow will again encircle the Earth perfectly, as it was in the beginning."

Alinta (Woman of the Fire) passed into Spirit on January 23, 2001. At the end she felt completion, in that she had been able to work diligently and successfully for many years at her core life task: helping to link the oldest culture on earth to the emerging global culture. She sowed seeds of hope and understanding.

Chapter Eleven

Blossoms in an Age of Flowers

While the notion that we live in a prophesied time of transition is accepted widely among native elders, the terms they use to describe the transition vary. Some elders say we are moving from the Fourth World to the Fifth World, as does Seneca grandmother Twylah Nitsch. Other wisdom keepers say we are moving into the world of the Sixth Sun, or the epoch of the 8th Fire. The Maya speak of the New Itza Age, some Christians see it as the Tribulation, astrologers call it the Age of Aquarius, Buddhists say it is Shambhala, and booksellers market it as the New Age. Yet another mythic descriptor—perhaps one with unifying attributes—is the Age of Flowers.

In his book *Beneath the Sun and Under the Moon,* Tony Shearer wrote that the calendars of the Native Americans offer neither specific descriptions nor hints about the character of the next epoch. So it may be. Those calendars were created in another time for the age that is closing, not for the one that may be dawning. But if we are indeed at the end of the time cycle marked by those calendars, and on the threshold of a new age, then it should be possible for perceptive souls to gain some sense of what character the emerging cycle will express.

PHOTO 25 *Ven. Dhyani Ywahoo.*
Photo by Pamela Cabel–Whiting
© 1986.

Ven. Dhyani Ywahoo has spent much time contemplating the calendars and the start of the new cycle. "For us," she says, "Harmonic Convergence was the ending of one fire and the start of a new fire—part of an ongoing cycle of change. According to the Native American calendar, we have entered a new cycle of Thirteen Heavens, a New Age in which we have the opportunity to let go of aggression and fear and begin to live a life of enlightened consciousness. The cycle that began in 1987 (Harmonic Convergence) created an opening in the mind's eye so we can see more clearly our unity. Lots of traditions were sharing. Many people came together and saw the common threads that bind us. The next step is to actually do it—to take the inner vision and make it real in the outer world through right action."

Dhyani is a teacher in the Etowah Cherokee tradition and also a recognized teacher of Tibetan Buddhism, in the Nyingma and Drikung Kagyu lineages. She teaches from a peace village deep in the heart of Vermont's Green Mountains, at the North end of the Appalachian mountain spine, along the Eastern flank of Turtle Island.

Dhyani says that many Native Americans have paid close attention to the transition described in the Native American calendar. "The age ending has been a time when people have gathered information about building and about inventions to make life better. Now it's time for people to recognize that the inventions are a creation of mind, to put aside such inventions as cause harm, and to bring forth and further develop those activities that benefit all beings and benefit the future generations."

"We are moving around the spiral, coming again to a place of whole civilization, of true planetary consciousness. What we see now are the fever throes, the end of the fever's nightmares as the sickness and poisons leave the system. Just how well the culture, the people, go through this time is really dependent upon the calling of the light, because in a time of purification the light makes clear the places of darkness.

"How much the planet will suffer, how much the people will suffer, is really determined by the consciousness of groups. It is no longer a matter of just individuals finding the light within themselves; it's really necessary to establish a network, to rebuild those areas of the Earth's web that have been harmed by unclear thinking.

"According to the way we are taught, and the seeds that are being planted, the new calendar that has begun is to manifest peace—an age of peace. The elders have asked—this is a large council of elders, so they speak to Central and North American people—that the morning after every full moon, at about 10 a.m., that we gather flowers and go outside and look to the Sun, to the flowers, and to the heart of the Earth. In so doing, we bring more solar energy and flower wisdom to the Earth, because the New Age is the Age of Flowers.

"Flowers give light and joy. They also have a very subtle consciousness. They have a unity of mind. Flower energy is peaceful, and flowers are great medicine. By meditation on flowers, we can reduce the inflammation caused by aggressive habits of mind. Flowers are our medicine for the next age. In this new time, flowers will become very significant as teachers and healers of humanity.

"Flowers move with the sun; thus they have a certain committed solar consciousness. They know the proper relationship between Spirit and Earth. The flowers remind us to look up to heaven and to actualize the solar energy in our own lives—to speak more clearly and to act more clearly.

"Flowers are the medicine we need for balance and tone. The old people say that when properly prepared—and some of the preparations can take as long as twelve years—flower essences can widen the frequency response of the human mind. They increase our sensitivity. But they need to be prepared with prayer, right offering, and dedication. Flowers can remove the poisons of incorrect thought and stir the body to its fullest health."

The Quickening
"Basically, these are still times for planting seeds of good relationship," Dhyani says. "Those who are responding to the teachings of the flowers are establishing a parallel government of people who are committed to peace and generating that energy."

According to Dhyani, one way the flowers are teaching humanity is through their pollen. In recent years, as the ozone has thinned and caused weakening of the human immune system, doctors have reported a sharp increase in the number of cases of hay fever, other allergies and asthma. As Dhyani explains, "Through the movement of flower pollen in the air, we are all being quickened. That quickening for some is frightening, and it also brings a reaction—just like when someone takes a homeopathic remedy. First, they may become a little bit sicker, but it's really the sickness being exaggerated so that the organism can be awakened to heal itself."

"The whole issue of allergy," she says, "is really an issue of the planetary system and not the human system. In some instances the Earth and the people are so out of alignment with one another that anything natural is disturbing to the human body. For years we've been taking artificial vitamins, and for years our food has been grown with artificial fertilizers. So the natural kingdom has been made an enemy, and the body and the immune system respond as if nature were an enemy. This is a result of years and years of improper drugging of the crops.

"I also think that's why there's so much of an increase in addictions among people. Because the plants are jazzed up, people get into the habit of being jazzed up. Then they start looking for more and more stimulants or depressants to continue that cycle. People who are in their forties today are the people who were eating in their formative years the most highly sprayed and the most highly chemically treated food that this world has ever seen. There's only so much that the human body can take.

"By releasing their pollen, flowers are trying to attract the attention of human beings. The plants do that specifically. Plants do have minds and they have alertness and consciousness," Dhyani says, "and they can change. Notice also that the atmosphere's quality is changing. Certainly there's less oxygen. There are more heavy metals and acid in the air. So the plants are working even harder to transmute these things, and in their efforts for transformation the plants that survive become more potent."

Dhyani and others have suggested that at some point a particular flower or flowers may be developed as healing potions—not so much for individuals, but rather for distressed areas of the planet. The preparation may be made and used as an offering to abused locations on the planet, such as old toxic waste sites, to help restore ecological balance.

If these planetary remedies are developed at some point during the Age of Flowers, Dhyani believes that the inner attitude of the people who offer the flowers will be critical. "It's not just the substance of the flower or the crystal or the water or anything," she explains, "it's also the intention with which these things are applied. It all needs the direction of clarified mind so that it can bring the result that is beneficial. That's why the elders always reminded us that prayer is important."

Jitterbug Perfume

In the late 1980s, best-selling author Tom Robbins published a novel entitled *Jitterbug Perfume*. The book contains a chapter with a peculiar title: Dannyboy's Theory (Where We Are Going and Why It Smells the Way It Does). In that chapter the fictional characters contend that humankind is about to enter the floral stage of evolutionary development.

Although the book is a novel, within the chapter Robbins offers some plain facts about human brains and the quality of their consciousness. Specifically, through his characters, he notes that reptile consciousness is cold, aggressive, self-preserving, angry, greedy, and paranoid. Neurophysicist Paul McLean has pointed out that within their skulls modern–day human beings still harbor a fully intact and functional reptilian brain: the limbic lobe, the hypothalamus, and perhaps other organs of the diencephalon. When we are in a cold sweat or a blind rage, he says, our reptile brain is in control of our consciousness.

Robbins points out that human beings also have a mammal brain, called the midbrain or mesencephalon, and that characteristics of mammal consciousness are warmth, generosity, loyalty, love, joy, grief, humor, pride, competition, and appreciation of art and music. In late mammalian times—the last several thousand years—human beings have developed a third brain, the telencephalon, consisting principally of the neocortex, a dense rind of nerve fibers about an eighth of an inch thick. This part of the brain is molded over the top of the existing mammal brain.

Brain researchers are greatly puzzled by the neocortex. What is its function? And why has it developed? In his book, Robbins concludes that the third brain is a floral brain, corresponding to the evolving stage of human development.

Flowers extract energy from light. Likewise, neuromelanin—one of the principal chemicals in this part of the brain—absorbs light and also has the capacity to convert light into other forms of energy. Consequently, Robbins notes, the neocortex is light sensitive and can itself be lit up by higher forms of mental activity, such as meditation or chanting. Thus, he notes, "the ancients were not being metaphoric when they referred to 'illumination.'" They were being literal.

In *Jitterbug Perfume*, Robbins asserts that we are moving gradually toward a dominant floral consciousness: "We require a less physically aggressive, less rugged human being now. We need a more relaxed, contemplative, gentle, flexible kind of person, for only he or she can survive (and expedite) this very new system that is upon us. Only he or she can participate in the next evolutionary phase. It has definite spiritual overtones, this floral phase of consciousness.

"Flowers do not see, hear, taste, or touch, but they react to light in a crucial manner, and they direct their lives and their environment through an orchestration of aroma...We live now in an information technology. Flowers have always lived in an information technology. Flowers gather information all day. At night, they process it. This is called photosynthesis.

"As our neocortex comes into full use, we, too, will practice a kind of photosynthesis. As a matter of fact, we already do, but compared to the flowers, our kind is primitive and limited. For one thing, information gathered from daily newspapers, soap operas, sales conferences, and coffee klatches is inferior to information gathered from sunlight. (Since all matter is condensed light, light is the source, the cause of life. Therefore, light is divine. The flowers have a direct line to God that an evangelist would kill for.)"

"With reptile consciousness," Robbins concludes, "we had hostile confrontation. With mammal consciousness, we had civilized debate. With floral consciousness, we'll have empathetic telepathy."

A Modality of Healing

Since the early part of the twentieth century, flowers have in fact emerged as an effective modality of healing. Specifically, in the late

1920s a British doctor began experimenting with flowers as remedies for human disease. The results of his experiments opened a whole new field of health care that began to blossom just as the 1980s were ending.

Edward Bach, M.D., (1886-1936) practiced traditional medicine from 1914 until 1918, when he became interested in homeopathy, the healing modality founded on the principle that like cures like: in other words, that small doses of whatever is causing a problem, intelligently applied, can bring about a positive healing reaction within the body.

Bach was an outstanding doctor, held in high regard by both orthodox and homeopathic physicians. In 1928, he became interested in flowers and began to prepare homeopathic remedies from various blossoms. As time went on, he observed excellent results from these medicines. Working steadily until the time of his death in 1936, he developed thirty-eight individual flower essences as well as the popular Rescue Remedy, a combination of several flowers used to alleviate trauma.

Bach believed that bodily ills were only symptoms. He wrote that the ills of the heart and the spirit should instead be the focus of a healer's attention: "It is our fears, our cares, our anxieties, and such like that open the path to the invasion of illness." Dr. Bach also believed that the overweening materialism of our times has caused us to focus almost exclusively on the physical aspects of disease and to pay scant attention to the underlying or spiritual causes.

In response to this perception, Bach developed a new branch of herbal and homeopathic medicine that employed flowers to relieve mental distress. With this system, problems could be dealt with on an inner level. Specifically, he created his flower remedies to heal attitudes such as anger, resentment, remorse, lack of confidence, greed, and anxiety. Bach believed that by correcting harmful mental attitudes, one could prevent a disease from becoming established in the body. If one treated a disease at the energy level, he posited, one could avoid having to deal with it later as a gross physical malady.

How the Flowers May Heal Us

Flower essences are part of an evolving branch of the healing arts known as vibrational medicine. With vibrational medicine the subtle energies of the human body are influenced gently and non-obtrusively, through means such as color, light, sound, fragrance, and the essences of flowers. The theory underlying these modalities is that all living things, including human beings, have energy that flows in and around the body in particular patterns. Those energy patterns are directly related to—and in fact may even be the mold for—the physical form of the body. Therefore, if one can bring a person's energy patterns (or energy bodies) into vitality and balance, then there will be a corresponding shift in the person's physical health.

As viewed from the perspective of the classical four elements (earth, fire, water and air), all of these healing approaches fall within the realm of air, specifically within the realm of Aquarius, which is the third and highest of the Zodiac's air signs. The figure of Aquarius is not pouring out water, but rather waves of air (energy). Aquarius has long been said to rule electricity, high technology, and flying of all kinds from jets to rockets. In human beings the Aquarian impulse is often expressed as a cool detached intellectualism, the scientific mind. Aquarius is yang, and can be exceedingly dry.

In the context of our times, one might well wonder, where does the yin or feminine energy come from to balance the yang–masculine energy of Aquarius. A likely response is, from the flowers—which are a yin expression of the Aquarian air impulse. Air–related healing modalities are based on the understanding that our state of health is a reflection of our alignment with the universal laws of truth, and the degree to which we are fulfilling our soul's destiny in a balanced way. The greater the integrity of our alignment, according to floral healing theory, the more easily our soul energies can radiate through us as good health or wholeness. In this understanding, illnesses or diseases are seen as outward manifestations of the different levels of tension that have accumulated within us. They reflect where we are out of alignment with the truth of our lives and the world.

One leading organization in the development of flowers as a healing modality has been the Alaskan Flower Essence Project. The project describes this aspect vividly: "Flowers," the project's brochures say, "are light patterns of truth, beautifully expressed in physical form."

Flowers are the highest, most beautiful, most refined part of plants. They are said to correspond to the human soul. Flower essences influence the subtle electrical energy field of the human body in much the same way acupuncture does, albeit more gently, and less obtrusively.

Flower essences are easy to prepare. All that is required is pure water, a glass bowl, sunlight, and fresh blossoms. The blossoms are harvested in a respectful way and then floated upon the water in the bowl and placed in the sunlight. The healing light of the sun helps transmit the particular energetic essence of the flowers into the water, potentizing it so it can be used for healing. The resulting flower essences are liquid plant preparations that convey the distinct imprint of the particular flower from which they are made. They expand a person's capacity to interweave the spiritual, mental, emotional, and physical aspects of wellness.

Dr. Bach developed remedies employing flowers such as Wild Rose, Clematis, Heather, Cherry Plum, Gorse, and Honeysuckle. In recent years, groups such as the Alaskan Flower Essence Project, the Flower Essence Society, Pegasus, and Perelandra have taken the art and science of healing with flowers much further. Their approach to healing through the personality of the patient has proven itself over and over, demonstrating the efficacy of flower essences in thousands of cases.

Flowers become an evolutionary force in the consciousness of the person who uses them. They are not the cause of the healing or the health that results from their use; rather, they are agents that support the free will and clear intention of the person who seeks to heal him or herself.

The Soul of Nature

Richard Katz and Patricia Kaminski are the founders of the Flower Essence Society (FES). Through this organizational vehicle, they support research and educational programs that deepen public understanding of flowers as a medium for healing.

FES teaches that flower essences address health in a broad sense by strengthening the link between body and soul. The organization professes that flowers can be used to treat a wide variety of disorders such as stress, addictions, depression, fear, emotional repression, and jealousy. They can also be used to enhance creativity and spiritual awareness.

"With flower essences," Richard Katz comments, "we are seeking to bring spiritual light into our lives. Forty years ago, with the nuclear explosion, we split apart matter to create light. Now the generation that was born in that time has matured and is deciding whether to continue to split apart matter to create light or to radiate it from within. Never has the choice been clearer."

If this is the Age of Flowers, and if flowers are to become our healers and teachers, then what have we got to learn? As Richard Katz sees it, "Flowers are the soul of nature, and they give it expression through color, form, and fragrance. Flower essences are the art and science of bringing the balance of nature to the human soul.

"Most remedies are intended to make us feel better, but flower essences can help us heal our souls and find our life direction. Perhaps the most healing experience you can have is to be aware of your life purpose."

To help a person develop awareness of and take steps toward ful-filling his or her life purpose, Katz recommends one of three specific flower essences, or a combination of all three: Mullein, Walnut, and Wild Oat. He suggests that the person place a few drops of the flower essences under the tongue and then relax, repeating this process rhyth-mically, several times a day for several weeks, to internalize the subtle qualities of the flowers. To strengthen the process, the person could also use affirmations, either of their own design or as suggested by a supplier of flower essences.

The Flower Essence Society has published a pioneering booklet on this theme, entitled *Affirmations: The Messages of the Flowers in Transform-ative Words for the Soul.* As the booklet explains, "Affirmations are a specialized activity within the larger field of meditation, contemplation and prayer. They are simple, directly evocative words which enable the soul to work toward positive, specific goals of inner development. It is a tenet of all spiritual teachings, as well as business and professional training programs, that the ordering of thought and the harmonizing of feeling has a powerful impact on our ability to manifest change, both within ourselves and within the word."

Affirmations are not magical words that immediately bring fortune or fame; rather, they are verbal tools that can help the personality to develop virtue and moral strength in accord with the real needs and capacities of the soul. Here, for example, are the original FES affir-mations for the three flower essences relating to life purpose:

Mullein
I hear the spiritual call that guides me.
I stand true to my inner guidance.
I bear aloft the torch of my Spirit Light.

Walnut

I am free of limiting influences.
I have the strength to follow inner guidance.
I break the chains that hinder my growth.

Wild Oat

I am clear in my life direction.
I express my soul's purpose in my life activities.
I create and attract the opportunities I need

Two other flower essences that are particularly appropriate to the times we live in are Iris and Mountain Pride. Iris was the Greek goddess of the rainbow, and the Iris flower is said to create a rainbow bridge in consciousness for humans, linking Earth with Spirit. Mountain Pride is a warrior flower; it builds strength and assertiveness in the face of great challenges. Together, Iris and Mountain Pride elevate the parts of the soul that are capable of confronting the enormous psychic, social, economic, and environmental shadows we have created for ourselves. They are flower essences well suited to Rainbow Warriors.

To gain a sense of how these flowers may help empower people who have been stirred by the mythology of the Rainbow Warriors, consider the original companion affirmations suggested by the Flower Essence Society.

Iris

I build a home between Earth and Spirit.
I work from the creative ground of my soul.
I nourish the world with my soul's rainbow light.

FIGURE 11. *Iris*

Mountain Pride

I am a spiritual warrior.
I meet obstacles and adversaries with fiery courage.
I cut through world darkness with the flaming sword
   of truth.

FIGURE 12. *Mountain Pride*

Many millions of people—from all the world's spiritual traditions—have a vivid sense that they have a particular destiny to fulfill at this juncture of world history—that it is their task to help steer the Earth somehow aright in this time of transition. For them the Age of Flowers may resonate as a mythic call to action—a call audible to the inner ear.

For the Children

The rising hills, the slopes,
of statistics
lie before us.
the steep climb
of everything, going up,
up, as we all
go down.

In the next century
or the one beyond that,
they say,
are valleys, pastures,
we can meet there in peace
if we make it.

To climb these coming crests
one word to you, to
you and your children:

stay together
learn the flowers
go light

—Gary Snyder, *Turtle Island* © 1974
Reprinted by permission of New Directions Publishing Corp.

Chapter Twelve

Ways of
a Spiritual Warrior

While the legend of the Rainbow Warriors is indigenous to Turtle Island, it has correlations in other parts of the world beyond America and Australia. One of the most striking correspondences is with the Shambhala Vision, a source of inspiration to the people of Tibet for more than twelve centuries.

As reported in my book, *Profiles in Wisdom: Native Elders Speak about the Earth,* Native Americans and Tibetans have an ancient and enduring connection. According to elders from both traditions, time-honored teachings hold that one day, when the balance of the people and the whole world is marked with strife and confusion, they will come together with others and work to restore peace, harmony, and spiritual awareness.

In her book *World as Lover, World as Self,* American author Joanna Macy tells the Tibetan version of this teaching, the Shambhala legend, as she learned it from Choegyal Rinpoche of the Tashi Jong Community in Northern India. What follows is a synopsis of the Shambhala vision as she recounts it.

Eventually, as the Earth evolves, there will come a time when all of life is threatened. Powerful political forces will rise in this time, forces that are predominantly barbarian—lacking discernment, refinement, and restraint. One power will be located in what is known today as the western hemisphere of the world, while the other will be located near the center of the Eurasian land mass. Even though the two great powers will have many similarities, they will fear each other and use their wealth to develop and maintain terrible weapons that have the potential to devastate all life.

At this precarious point in history, Shambhala will begin to emerge. Shambhala will not be a place, but rather an understanding that lives in the hearts and minds of some of the people, the Shambhala warriors. These warriors will wear no uniforms and carry no flags; they will have no land base of their own. They will move, instead, on the terrain of the barbarians.

When Shambhala begins to emerge, the Shambhala warriors will have to live with exalted physical and moral courage, for their task will be to enter the heart of the barbarian powers, to walk the corridors of power where the decisions are made, and to dismantle the thoughts and weapons of destruction. They will do this successfully because they will know that the problems and weapons have been made by the human mind, and thus they can be unmade. The Shambhala warriors will see clearly that the threat to life on Earth comes not from outer space or a remote, satanic figure, but from the very decisions and lifestyles people have chosen.

As Macy reports, Choegyal Rinpoche said that the Shambhala warriors will have only two weapons to aid them in their struggle: compassion and insight. Compassion will give them the energy, the will, and the power to take action. Insight will guide them to apply this energy with intelligence and skill.

In her first book, *Despair and Personal Power in the Nuclear Age,* Macy wrote of how the overwhelming troubles in the world can cause people to shut down, to become numb, and to bury themselves in diversions and entertainment in an attempt to avoid sorrow. In essence, people dread confronting the feelings of despair they harbor in response to personal and world conditions. And yet, as she concludes, "at the prospect of the extinction of civilization, feelings of grief and horror are natural."

The tendency to refuse the natural experience of sorrow exacts a steep price. It impoverishes the emotional and sensory life of people, and dulls the energy essential for survival and true joy in life. Our despair, Macy has written, must be acknowledged and worked through. Only in this way can the potent emotional currents of this very natural human response be tapped and then expressed in the world as helpful action.

While compassion may give the Shambhala warriors energy to act, it is risky. It can lead to emotional and psychic burn out. For that reason, Shambhala warriors also need insight; in particular, they need an understanding that all of life is connected, all interrelated in what Native American elders often refer to as the Sacred Hoop of life.

This teaching is far more than mystical whimsy. Modern physics and mathematics have advanced the understanding that matter and energy are interchangeable and, ultimately, both woven into a single unified field. Everything really is connected, and everything is in dynamic flux. The universe is "a single, unbroken wholeness in flowing movement," as described by physicist David Bohm. The Algonquin words *Manitou* and *Gitchee Manitou* describe a similar, if not the same, understanding. They refer not a Supreme Being, as in Western spiritual conceptions, but rather to a cosmic, mysterious power existing everywhere in nature, and connecting all things.

Scientists say this universal connection occurs at the level of the Planck scale, wherein the scale of measurement is to the atom as the atom is in scale to the solar system. What happens to any one part of the vast field of matter and energy which is our reality (the Sacred Hoop) affects all other parts.

Eunice Baumann-Nelson, Ph.D., of the Penobscot Nation, is but one Native American elder who has noted the intersection of the unified-field theories of Western science with the Sacred Hoop concept of aboriginal philosophy: "This is a stunning insight…From it I know that I have the responsibility of caring for you and all things that exist as I care for myself. I have to behave as if everything I do to you and Creation, I do to myself. Because that's the way it is. That's reality. Consequently, it behooves me to act with respect and love."

Our personal connection with each other and with all of nature is thus not a nostalgic or romantic notion, but is as accurate a worldview as modern physics and mathematics can ascertain at the start of the 21st Century. This worldview—anciently indigenous to Turtle Island and Tibet by way of insight and contemplation, and now joined by the leading edge of Western science—is so far grasped by only a few people. Over time many more people may come to appreciate it. If so, they may naturally employ it as a foundation for decisions and actions.

Spiritual warriors who explore and honor this universal linkage soon recognize that life is not an eternal battle between good and some external evil. Rather, as Choegyal Rinpoche expressed it, "good and evil run through the landscape of every human heart." Through discipline and prayer, harmful or evil impulses can be transcended.

Spiritual warriors learn that their actions—when undertaken with pure intent—have repercussions throughout the web of life. Even small deeds such as recycling soda bottles, forgiving a transgressor, or planting an organic garden, have ramifications far beyond what we are capable of knowing or measuring. Everything is connected. Everything matters.

The Sacred Path of the Warrior

Some people hold the concept of warrior to be noble, even glorious, and they revel in accounts of history's epic battles. For others, seeing how much suffering has come to the world as the result of conflict and battle, the concept of warrior is repugnant. Clearly the concept is in need of redefinition that people can agree upon. As a prelude for reconsidering the concept, we'd do well to ponder the foundation of the matter: a warrior's true and ultimate responsibility is to protect family and, by extension, all the people. Sometimes that is essential, inescapable. But how can this best be done?

As understood in the legend of the rainbow warriors and in the Shambhala vision, spiritual warriors do no harm, inflict no pain, cause no suffering. They work to set things right by good example. That, ultimately, is what works.

In a time when many people are storing up knives, guns and bullets to defend against the gathering clouds of a fearful future, spiritual warriors take a different tack. Warriorship for them in no way entails aggression on others; rather, it means having integrity, being brave, and standing skillfully and forthrightly—but peacefully—for all that supports life. The war is for safety, sanity, respect.

The late, highly controversial Tibetan Rinpoche Chögyam Trungpa (1940-1987), lived and worked in North America for many years. In his remarkable book, *Shambhala: The Sacred Path of the Warrior,* he offered a series of essays on what it means to be a spiritual warrior.

As Trungpa wrote, "The Shambhala teachings are founded on the premise that there is basic wisdom that can help solve the world's problems. This wisdom does not belong to any one culture or religion, nor does it come only from the West or the East." Rather, it is a tra-

PHOTO 28. *Chögyam Trungpa Rinpoche. Photo by Martin Janowitz from the collection of the Vajradhatu Archives.*

dition of wisdom that has existed in many cultures at many times throughout history, and has often been expressed by people, including warriors. Some speak of this as the Perennial Wisdom.

Based on the inspiration of Chögyam Trungpa's writings—and on the counsel of other learned elders from around the world—I offer the following compendium of insights and observations about the spiritual path.

Compendium of Wisdom Teachings

Be interested in life. As any elderly person will tell you, life passes quickly. Each of us has only a few brief cycles of time to experience and to contribute. When you pay attention to the people and the natural world around you, boredom evaporates and you develop the capacity to experience a raw delight in being alive.

Allow yourself to be authentic. There's no need to put on airs, either to boast or to denigrate yourself for what you have done or what you cannot do. No good will come from exaggerating your potential or ignoring your shortcomings. Release doubt or hesitation about being yourself. Relax: you are who you are. When you fear or obsess about yourself and the problems of the world, you become selfish. You want to build fortifications in yourself and your home so you can fend off the world. This helps not at all. From being open and honest with yourself, you learn to be open and honest with others.

Cultivate who you are as a human being. Fully engage the truth you find in your heart. Be gentle with yourself and discover your own basic goodness. Take time to deliberately discover who you are and what you inherently have to offer. Accurate and compassionate self-appraisal is essential; it creates the ground for helping yourself and then others.

Acknowledge your fears of yourself, others, and the world, and then go beyond them. Everyone experiences fear; it's a basic human condition. True bravery does not mean eliminating fear; it means confronting the fear and then going beyond it.

Recognize that sadness, even deep grief, are likely to be a part of your response to world conditions. How can anyone look upon the homelessness, the pollution, and the corruption, and not feel grief. To deny this grief is to repress a profoundly powerful source of energy.

Discover that satisfaction and the real goodness of life come from appreciating simple experience. When you see the sunrise or a baby's smile, when you hear a bird sing, taste a savory morsel, or feel the wind freshen your skin, take time to acknowledge and appreciate this beauty. This enriches your life, and makes it possible for you to extend this fundamental goodness out into the world in other ways.

Foster a sense of thanksgiving. This concept is also a primary Native American teaching. In the way of Turtle Island, people do not so much pray for things they want, as they direct their thoughts and words in gratitude for the gifts they already have: another day to live, sunshine, rain, food, flowers, friendship. When we appreciate the world, we don't make a mess in it with what we say or do.

Find and follow your own vision. If you allow yourself to become trapped in an activity, occupation, or relationship that leaves unfulfilled the calling of your heart, you will feel frustrated and unhappy. The calling of your heart may not lead you to fame and fortune, but it will guide you to make an important contribution to the world, and to satisfaction.

Renounce barriers between yourself and others. This is the spiritual warrior's act of supreme courage. When you make yourself more available and more open to other people, you will find your experience to be full and exquisitely vivid. This is both your gift to life, and your reward for being alive.

Consider that little is to be gained by creating an enemy and conquering him or her to make yourself feel better. Every human being has good and bad attributes. Rather than focussing solely upon what you deem as bad in the world, what can you do to support what you see as good and helpful.

Look beyond appearance and strive to grasp the essence of the people you meet. Some are handsome and some are grotesque, some are rich and some are poor, some are clean and some are dirty. But those are all outer circumstances. What lies below the surface?

Celebrate Life. As you learn to appreciate the basic goodness of life—in warmth, human feeling, colors, and so forth—you will naturally develop a sense of upliftment. Express this in celebrations of ritual and ceremony, according to the traditions of your heart. When you sing, dance, and pray with others, you give something back to life rather than just taking. This helps to keep the balance of nature, and to knit families and communities together.

Cultivate good humor. Some people, upon discovering a truth they feel the world needs, become so passionate that they are willing to kill or to die for it; they beat their ideas and themselves into others, and eventually into the ground. Yet other people threaten to commit suicide because they aren't getting what they think they deserve out of life. Lighten up. A genuine sense of good humor means having a light touch as you deal with yourself and reach out to the world.

Respect your body as the physical home of your spirit. Entire libraries of books have been written on the themes of good nutrition, fresh air, and regular exercise; most carry worthwhile messages. Spiritual warriors require a foundation of good health maintained with a diet of simple, clean food. In the same vein, respect the Earth as the physical home of humanity's collective spirit.

Pay attention to farms and farming. In the modern world farmers are our ambassadors to the Earth. In return for their attentions—whether enlightened or exploitive—the Earth gives us the food we eat. This is our fundamental linkage to life and to the future. All who eat have a basic responsibility to see that this link is clear and wholesome.

Avoid sloppiness in your personal appearance, home, and work. These reveal and intensify feelings of depression, hopelessness, and futility. Everything worth doing is worth doing well.

Sit and stand erectly; breathe fully and consciously. When you slouch, you cannot breath properly, and this is the beginning of neurosis. Your posture is an outward expression of your soul's relationship between heaven and Earth. Habitual slouching scrambles the flow of energy. When you sit and stand with dignity, you proclaim to yourself and to the world that you are going to be a warrior, fully present, fully human. When you breathe fully, you engage with life fully in the present.

Synchronize your mind and body. As Chögyam Trungpa writes, "this is not a concept or a random technique someone thought up for self-improvement. Rather, it is a basic principle of how to be a human being, and of how to use your mind and body together." This principle involves seeing, hearing, and feeling fully and carefully, so that your responses will be based on reality, not what you have imagined.

Tell the truth. Shed any hesitation about maintaining an attitude of fundamental honesty concerning the way things are, and what is happening around you. Falsehood at any level smears the world with confusion and conflict. Only truth can clear this away. Spiritual warriors bear witness to the truth, without malice. When you tell the truth to others, you create an opportunity for them to express themselves honestly as well.

Speak gently and directly. Spiritual warriors neither bark nor whine. Firm but gentle speech expresses your inherent dignity, and carries true authority.

Extend respect to the whole circle of life. If you want the respect of other people, you must respect them—even though you may not like them. True humility means recognizing that everyone you meet has something to teach you. Likewise, respect the soil, the air, the water, and all the creations—even unto the earthworms—that make your life possible.

Touch the Earth. For maximum physical and mental health, make physical contact with the Earth. When you touch your hands, bare feet, or body to the land, you establish a necessary bioelectric circuit with the blue–green planet that provides all your food, water, shelter, and even the atoms that make up your body. This is analogous to the life–energy connection you had with your mother while you lived in her womb. By making conscious contact with the physical Earth, you bring your-self naturally and gently into harmony with it. As experience will show, touching the breast of the Earth Mother regularly, and in a sacred manner yields nurturance and stability—two foundational elements of a healthy life. They are also elements that help to counterbalance the stress and speed of modern times.

Find a way to slow down. As David Gehue of the MiqMaq Nation advised when he spoke at UN Headquarters, Native American elders have been saying for some time that the world is going to go faster and faster; consequently the human beings need to find ways to slow down if they are to live in a healthy manner amidst this speed. That way may be a regular walk in the forest, meditation, yoga, a hot bath, playing a musical instrument, or any other form which allows you to feel rou-tinely centered and peaceful. This is essential for good physical and mental health.

Maintain your balance in the face of either good or bad news. Exaggerated responses to success or failure, whether personal or global, will throw you off balance. The spiritual warrior seeks to be solidly rooted, and to trust in his or her heart. Bad news and failures are acknowledged and examined; good news and success are appreciated. Life goes on.

Work with your life situation as it is now. The past is over; the future is not here yet. The spiritual warrior does not divert energy by longing for additional gifts, opportunities, or resources, but works with what is at hand, step by step.

Honor the elders. Throughout history, every successful culture has honored its older members. Age conveys the benefit of experience, and in many cases experience leads to wisdom. By listening carefully and respectfully to what elders say, you may benefit from the wisdom they represent. In turn, the elders will realize that their lives still have important meaning for their culture. The accumulated experience of elders offers the context and wherewithal for the enthusiasm of young people. If young people see that old age is a barren time of isolation, illness and neglect, they will lack enthusiasm for life.

Heed the Seven Generations teaching. The Seven Generations principle—as articulated by the Haudenausenee peoples—expresses a nearly universal aspect of Native American philosophy. Before you make a major decision or take a major action, reflect. Who were your parents, grandparents, and great grandparents, unto seven generations of your ancestral lineage? Who are your children, or the children in your life? Who will their children be, and the children of those children, unto seven future generations. When you are sure your actions and decisions will honor the past, and also safeguard the future for seven generations, then proceed in good conscience.

Honor the wisdom tradition of your family. You were born into a particular family and wisdom tradition for a reason. Though your parents may not have followed it, and though you may not feel called to follow it, there is something there for you to learn. Only by examining your family roots and traditions can you master the lessons.

Regard your family and home as sacred, no matter how humble or grand. Otherwise you create a huge gap between your vision for society and the reality of your everyday existence. The only way to implement your vision for society is to begin by bringing it down to your family and your household. The appreciation of sacredness begins with taking a respectful interest in details—the cooking of food, the washing of dishes, the changing of diapers, and so forth. An enlightened society rests on the foundation of enlightened families and homes.

Remember that a warrior's true job is to protect the people. Of necessity, this implies protecting your territory—the Earth—and supporting it so that it may bring forth an abundance of clean food and water. Without this, no warrior can claim to have protected the people in general, or their family in particular.

Look beyond yourself and your home to see how you can help the world. This is a basic human responsibility, and a privilege.

Work ceaselessly to be an example of rightness in your life and career, without being righteous about it. Nothing is quite so irritating to others as sanctimony and self-righteousness. What can you do to improve yourself and your work in the world?

Develop a specific set of skills. High ideas and good intentions are of little value unless they are harnessed to skill and discipline. Whether you are a teacher, a healer, a homemaker, a farmer, a webmaster, an environmentalist, or a builder, you must master the techniques that will allow you to do your work effectively.

Learn to see yourself as more than your job or your role in the world. Not everyone has a paid job fulfilling their heart's desire. Still, at work or outside work, you can make an important contribution. In this, quantity is far less important than quality.

Check the impulse to abuse power. Everyone develops some power as a human being, and consequently has the opportunity to wield that power, either positively or negatively. You can see this in relationships and careers, as well as in the arts, sciences, and government. When they seek power or a vision, the Lakota people often pray in this way: "I ask this not for myself alone, but so the people may live." A similar prayer will help you to anchor your ego so it does not get out of hand.

Avoid the temptation of imposing your ideas and philosophy on others. This is high arrogance, based upon fundamental insecurity about yourself and your view of truth. Ideological aggression only creates additional resentment and chaos in the world. Some people think the world needs capitalism, other think it needs communism or a particular religious theory like Christianity or Buddhism. But when ideas are pushed upon people, it constitutes a grievous violation of free will. If you are living a wise life, if your ideas have merit, trust that other people will recognize this and that, of their free will, they support you and your efforts.

Sit in a Circle. The council circle is a time–honored way of ensuring that everyone is seen and heard, and that all the people have a chance to place their "good mind" on the question at hand. When challenges arise in your family, workplace, or community, gather in a circle with all the people who are directly concerned. In the council circle, each person speaks in turn and then listens silently and respectfully to all others. There is no debate. There are only layers of discussion. The circle is an especially helpful social form in times of great change.

Ponder first, then dare. Carefully consider the challenges before you, applying intelligence, intuition, and prayer; then act. The late American President Theodore Roosevelt put this teaching into a memorable state-ment: "Far better it is to dare mighty things, to win glorious triumphs, even though checkered by failure, then to take rank with those poor spirits who neither enjoy much nor suffer much, because they live in the gray twilight that knows not victory nor defeat."

Refuse to give up on anyone or anything worthwhile, including yourself. Each of us has problems, and the world itself, clearly, has great problems. Spiritual warriors recognize that steady effort brings results. We can, ultimately, build an enlightened society. But this requires great courage.

Ponder your mortality. You will die some day. What will your legacy be? How will you be remembered?

Bear in mind that wisdom is not some monumental thing outside yourself. You are related to all things, including the inherent wisdom and goodness of the universe. Being a Rainbow Warrior is not a program or a set of techniques that you apply when an obstacle arises or when you are unhappy, it is a continual journey. To be a warrior in this way is to strive to be genuine in every moment of your life, to stand for the Earth, and to take joy in the journey.

Epilogue

"A vision without a task is a dream. A task without a vision is drudgery. But a vision with a task can change the world."

—BLACK ELK

All these tales and much more, this is the Legend of the Rainbow Warriors. Once again, in yet another way, the stories have been told. Readers must ask, is the telling enough? Is the telling true? Did our native ancestors have a worthy vision of the Rainbow Warriors and of a new era? In what ways might those visions serve us today?

The cumulative evidence that we are in a time of profound change is unmistakable. Even political leaders invoke phrases such as New World Order, though they give scant definition of what they mean. By any estimation, planetary upheaval surrounds us on all fronts, and many thousands of people have joined their efforts and resources on behalf of the Earth, whether they think of themselves as Rainbow Warriors or not. But does any of this make the myths real?

I stake no special claim of ultimate truth for the perspective shared in this book. It's a story. The voices, both ancient and modern, are authentic: the myths are recounted as faithfully as possible, and the current affairs are accurate and verifiable from standard references. But how, in the end, shall the reader put them together?

While I will venture no bold assertion of ultimate truth for the conclusions suggested by this book, I will say this: they are part of my truth. I offer the *Legend of the Rainbow Warriors* in the hope that it will raise helpful questions for you, the reader: What lies beneath the surface? What gives your life its meaning? What is your myth? How are you acting to make your myth a living part of the world's experience? If the legend of the rainbow warriors speaks to you, what can you do to make it real, to engage more directly in the ancient quest of heroes and heroines: bringing heaven to Earth?

Today, as ever, we face the present and the future. According to the mythology of Harmonic Convergence, we are in a critical twenty-five-year epoch of change—change that is more far–reaching and enigmatic than at any other time in history. The necessity for taking meaningful action, therefore, bears upon us not in ten years, or even next year, but now. The event known as Harmonic Convergence can, in a certain light, be understood as the start of a time when every human being is called to awaken as a Rainbow Warrior: someone who lives with respect for and in support of all of the creations on Earth. The final date on the ancient calendars of the Americas—December 21, 2012—draws near.

The world events that occurred in apparent connection with Harmonic Convergence are rapidly altering our worldview. We can see ever more clearly that our planet is but a mote of dust in a vast universe, and that we have far more to learn about ourselves and the spiral of our neighborhood galaxy, the Milky Way. As we recognize this connection more distinctly through science and expanding spiritual perception, we can grasp more fully that we are part of a vast, ordered universe.

By the year of this new edition of *Legend of the Rainbow Warriors,* it is apparent that the fire element is wildly out of balance upon our earth. This is evident in mounting stockpiles of nuclear weapons and waste, via the inundation of ultraviolet (UV) radiation from the sun streaming ever more ferociously through the widening hole in the earth's protective ozone layer, and in mounting evidence of the Greenhouse Effect, as it steadily heats the earth. This fire energy needs to be swiftly and skillfully controlled where it is wreaking havoc, and then be sagely directed to yield both warmth and illumination.

This book is in no way an attempt to put any individual elder, or native culture itself, on a pedestal. That kind of separation would be a grave mistake. The elders and the culture they are part of are altogether human, with both the best and worst implications of that term. Native American culture is still in recovery from 500 years of genocidal assault, and from the faith–shattering experience of having 428 treaties broken or violated by the US government and various states (every single treaty ever written, without exception). On reservations, drug, alcohol, gambling, and nutrition problems are widespread. The Red Nations have a long way to go to complete their recovery. But the Sacred Fire has been kindled again in many nations, many hearts. In my view, our Native American relatives hold some crucial understandings that are part of their culture. They have medicine to heal the earth. Prayer, ceremony, and the Seventh Generation teaching are parts of the medicine. This, I contend, is neither sentimentality nor superstition, but rather a spiritual fact.

Cherokee and Buddhist teacher Dhyani Ywahoo puts the issue this way: "We are moving around the spiral, coming again to a place of whole civilization, of true planetary consciousness. What we see now are the fever throes, the end of the fever's nightmares as the sickness and poisons leave the system. It is a mistake to focus on the fever; instead, we need to focus on the means of healing."

A crucial aspect of the means of healing will be for the leading institutions of our global civilization—science, technology, manufacturing, and so forth—to fundamentally redirect themselves in light of reality. Their models of progress and development endanger Mother Earth. The planet requires our immediate and wise ministrations; to provide that attention, our institutions require a broader, wiser vision.

"This vision," environmental writer Diane Dumanoski has suggested, "needs to unmask the deepest assumptions of the current order, many of them rather recent philosophical inventions. This means taking on the guiding myths of modern life—notions that are so much a part of the current worldview that many people take them to be truths rather than assumptions." When the operative myths of modern life are clearly discerned, they may be acknowledged as jaundiced in possibilities.

One powerful modern myth has been formed by advertising images of vast, luxurious wealth—the myth of materialism; another has been formed by the bloody, sorrowful images that pervade movies, music and computer games—the myth that the world is hate–filled and chaotic beyond redemption. For many millions of people, in the absence of something more wholesome, such barren or noxious visions have become their personal working myths, albeit often unconsciously. They lie beneath the surface. The legend of the rainbow warriors offers an alternative of hope and happy possibility based upon personal responsibility.

The New World Order we hear politicians speak of seems, to many, either vaguely or implicitly ominous. Perhaps this is because, lacking clear definition, the New World Order appears to consist of vast, impersonal government bureaucracies, interlocking and unknowable financial networks, multinational corporations with allegiance only to profit, the loss of personal privacy, and the advance of sophisticated technologies without regard to their consequences. This is not what most people want. We cannot help but wonder about the places of the individual and the family in this context.

Likewise, many people, particularly from fundamentalist traditions, have been fearful of the myths of the new age and the rainbow. They sense in these myths a threat to what they hold sacred. As someone who has explored and reported on these facets of our world for nearly twenty–five years, I have also, on occasion, seen cause for concern: individuals and groups who were headed in what I take as manipulative, naive, or impractical directions, or those who are focused narrowly on profit. On occasion, when people have surrendered their powers of discernment or free will to others, I have seen tragedy. These have been exceptions. Most of what I have seen has been wholesome, respectful, and empowering.

What might be called the New Age movement is not ultimately about crystals or channeling, it has no central leader or organization; control and hierarchy, in fact, are its antithesis. Rather, the rainbow new age myth, as I hear it, is about personal sovereignty: individual liberty to be who you are while willingly accepting responsibility for self, family, community, and planet—coupled with recognition that all these elements are inextricably bound together in a web of relationships that can be, depending upon how we weave it, ugly or beautiful.

Folksinger Bob Dylan put it cannily many years ago when, with irony, he sang, "Don't follow leaders, watch your parking meters." The rainbow movement, to the extent that it is a movement, is as decentralized and as diverse as the human community. It's about people following their personal visions, and offering the gift of their visions to the larger community of life on the planet. Whether they think of themselves as Christian, Moslem, Buddhist, Jewish, Native American, or in some other way, rainbow warriors recognize the fundamental necessity of respecting differences, and honoring the Earth we share.

No doubt some readers will regard the *Legend of the Rainbow Warriors* as a grade–B fantasy and scoff at the notion that there is any credible verification for such a hopeful and holistic worldview. To these readers I say, study the texts of science. Read what the leading physicists, mathematicians, and biologists are saying now about the nature of reality and the fundamental fact of our connectedness. Study the revelations of quantum mechanics, relativity, chaos theory, and superstrings. There is far more evidence to support the emerging holistic philosophies of a new age, than there is to buttress the widely held belief that we are separate from other aspects of creation and that we live our lives as individuals, unaffected by dreams, untouched by mystery. In the contrast of these worldviews, there is paradox—paradox that may well occupy forward–thinking people for generations to come.

As I understand the myth, the rainbow warriors are not likely to come charging onto the scene like the cavalry to save us, nor should we hold our breath waiting for them to arrive en masse from parts unknown. The rainbow warriors are here already, and we are they. That is, we are if we choose to be, no matter the color of our skin or the name of our religion. Out of our diversity, we find strength and unity. This is an essential part of the legend of the rainbow warriors: the understanding that every facet and shade of the rainbow is necessary for its integrity and beauty.

In North America, we have long cherished the myth of the melting pot. Out of the many diverse cultures streaming onto this continent and weaving themselves together, one new race of people would ultimately emerge. Could that melting pot be the one at the end of the rainbow?

The future will be whatever we make of it. What myth will we follow? What dream will we pursue for ourselves, our children, and our grandchildren unto seven generations? These are questions we would do well to engage as we move beyond the millennium.

If you count yourself among the Rainbow Warriors, then realize that you may not always be called to glorious tasks before the public eye. The rainbow bridge to a new world is built each day through hard work and the seemingly small decisions we all make. Can you find a non-polluting detergent for washing your clothes? Can you install a solar water heater? Can you plant an organic garden, or support a local farmer? Will you treat the plants and animals with respect? Will you find and follow your vision? Will you remember the Earth as you make your nightly prayers? Can you help your family, neighbors, or community to grow in some way? With such small, steady steps is myth made real.

If the myth of Daedalus can come to life as a human being spreads synthetic wings and soars over the sea using only the strength of his body for power, and if the myth of space travel can propel humans to walk on the moon, then the Legend of the Rainbow Warriors and the myth of a new age can also become real. This much is certain. We can, if we choose, protect and defend our Mother Earth, and encircle her with a rainbow culture of integrity, beauty and spiritual prosperity.

— *The End* —

Resources

In general readers will find a wealth of additional information about the people, topics, and events mentioned in Legend of the Rainbow Warriors by searching the World Wide Web. To guide readers interested in further study, some specific resources are offered below:

AmyLee
P.O. Box 550
Zoar, OH 44697
www.hernative roots.com
www.sisterhoodoftheshields.net

José and Lloydine Argüelles
www.tortuga.com

Brooke Medicine Eagle
c/o Singing Eagle Enterprises
PMB C401
One 2nd Ave. East
Polson, MT 59860
www.MedicineEagle.com

Dream Maker Bison Ranch
(Home of Miracle Moon and Rainbow Spirit, two white buffaloes)
12244 Buffalo Butte Lane
Custer, SD 57730
www.janetkierstead.com/w.htm

DaVal's (Heider) Family Farm
(Home of Miracle, the first white buffalo)
2739 S. River Rd
Janesville, WI 53546
www.whitemiracle.com

Greenpeace
702 H St. NW
Washington, DC 20001
www.greenpeaceusa.org

Scott Guynup
Illustrator, Visionary Artist
707 Brunswick Drive
Waynesville, NC 28786

Manitonquat (Medicine Story)
Mettanokit Community
c/o Another Place
173 Merriam Hill Rd.
Greenville, NH 03048

Corrine McLaughlin and Gordon Davidson
The Center for Visionary Leadership
3408 Wisconsin Avenue, NW Suite 200
Washington, DC 20016
www.visionarylead.org

Hunbatz Men
Communidad Indigena Maya pdo. Postal 7-013
Mérida, Yucatán, México.
E-mail: mayan@avantel.net

Heyoka Merrifield (artist, sculptor, jeweler)
c/o Heyoka's Studio
P.O. Box 70
Stevensville, MT 59870
www.heyoka-art.com

Brant Secunda
Dance of the Deer Foundation
P.O. Box 699
Soquel, CA 95073
www.shamanism.com

Oh Shinnah
c/o Four Directions Foundation
P.O. Box 2676
Columbia Falls, MT 59912

Sun Bear (deceased, but his Medicine Society remains active)
Bear Tribe Medicine Society
3750–A Airport Boulevard #223
Mobile, Alabama 36608–1618

Twylah Nitsch
c/o Seneca Indian Historical Society
P.O. Box 2313
Orange Park, FL 32067–2313

Ven. Dhyani Ywahoo
c/o Sunray Meditation Society
P.O. Box 269
Bristol, VT 05443
www.sunray.net

World Peace & Prayer Day (June 21 every year)
World Peace Day Office
P.O. Box 952
Hill City, SD 57745
www.worldpeaceday.com

*The Cry of the Earth conference discussed in Chapter 8 was documented on video-
tape. For information contact either of these two organizations:*

The Wittenberg Center for Alternative Resources
188 Wittenberg Rd.
Bearsville, NY 12409
www.wittenbergcenter.org

The Crescentera Foundation
459 Columbus Ave., Suite 201
New York, NY 10024

*From the Heart of the World: The Elder Brothers' Warning, Alan Ereira, 1991.
The only outside contact with the Kogi: the last surviving pre-Columbian civilization
of South America. (video documentary available from Mystic Fire Videos).*

Floral Resources

Alaskan Flower Essence Project
P.O. Box 1369
Homer, AK 99603
www.alaskanessences.com

Aveda
400 Pheasant Ridge Drive
Blaine, MN 55449
800–328–0849
www.aveda.com

Bach Flower Remedies
Bach/Ellon USA, Inc.
644 Merric Rd.
Lynbrook, NY 11563

Flower Essence Society
P.O. Box 459
Nevada City, CA 95959
800–736–9222
www.flowersociety.org

Bibliography

Arguelles, Jose. *Mayan Factor: Path Beyond Technology.* Santa Fe, NM: Bear & Company, 1987.

Balin, Peter. *The Flight of the Feathered Serpent.* Wilmot, WI: Arcana Publishing Co., 1978.

Bloom, Harold and Rosenberg, David. *Book of J.* (Translated from the Hebrew by Rosenberg, interpreted by Harold Bloom). New York: Vintage Books, 1991.

Boissiere, Robert. *The Return of Pahana: A Hopi Myth.* Santa Fe, NM: Bear & Company, 1990.

Brown, Dee. *Bury My Heart at Wounded Knee.* New York: Washington Square Press, 1970.

Brown, Joseph Epes. *The Sacred Pipe: Black Elk's Account of the Seven Rites of the Oglala Sioux.* Middlesex, England: Penguin Books, 1953.

Brown, Michael, and John May. *The Greenpeace Story.* London: Dorling Kindersley, Ltd., 1989.

Brown, Vinson. *Voices of Earth and Sky: The Vision Life of the Native Americans.* Happy Camp, CA: Naturegraph Publishers, Inc., 1974.

Buenfil, Alberto Ruz. *Rainbow Nation Without Borders: Toward an Ecotopian Millennium.* Santa Fe, NM: Bear & Company, 1991.

Campbell, Joseph. *The Hero with a Thousand Faces.* Princeton, NJ: Princeton University Press, 1956.

Campbell, Joseph. *Myths to Live By.* New York: Viking Books, 1972.

Chinmoy, Sri. *Kundalini: The Mother–Power.* Jamaica, NY: Aum Publications, 1974.

Dumanoski, Diane. *Rethinking Environmentalism,* E Magazine, December, 1998

Eagle, Brooke Medicine. *Buffalo Woman Comes Singing.* New York, Ballentine, 1993.

Eagle, Brooke Medicine. *The Last Ghost Dance: A Guide for Earth Mages.* New York, Ballentine. 2000.

Eliade, Mircea (translated by Trask, Willard R.). *Myth of the Eternal Return, or Cosmos and History.* Princeton, NJ: Princeton University Press, 1991.

Ereira, Alan *The Elder Brothers.* New York: Vintage Books,1993.

Fox, Matthew. *Original Blessing.* Santa Fe, NM: Bear & Company, 1983.

Hand, Floyd Looks for Buffalo. *Learning Journey on the Red Road.* Learning Journey Communications, Toronto, Canada, 1998.

Iron Thunderhorse and Donn Le Vie, Jr. *Return of the Thunderbeings.* Santa Fe., NM: Bear & Company, 1990.

Kaiser, Rudolf. *The Voice of the Great Spirit: Prophecies of the Hopi Indians.* Boston, MA: Shambhala Publications, Inc., 1991.

Kaminski, Patricia, and Richard Katz. *Affirmations: The Messages of the Flowers in Transformative Words for the Soul.* Nevada City, CA: Flower Essence Society, 1989.

Macy, Joanna. *Despair and Personal Power in the Nuclear Age.* Philadelphia, PA: New Society publishing, 1983.

Macy, Joanna. *World as Lover, World as Self.* Berkeley, CA: Parallax Press, 1991.

McGaa, Ed Eagle Man. Rainbow Tribe: *Ordinary People Journeying on the Red Road.* New York, NY, Harper Collins, 1992.

McFadden, Steven. *Profiles in Wisdom: Native Elders Speak about the Earth.* Santa Fe, NM: iuniverse.com, 2000.

McLaughlin, Corrine and Gordon Davidson. *Spiritual Politics: Changing the World from the Inside Out,* New York, Ballentine, 1994.

Men, Hunbatz. *Secrets of Mayan Science/Religion*. Santa Fe, NM: Bear & Company, 1990.

Merrifield, Heyoka. *Eyes of Wisdom: the Myth of White Buffalo Woman*. Rainbird Publishers (P.O. Box 70, Stevensville, MT 59870), 1997.

Needleman, Jacob. *The Way of the Physician*. New York: Harper & Row, 1985.

Neihardt, John G. *Black Elk Speaks*. New York: William Morrow and Co., 1932.

Ovanson, David. *The Secret Architecture of Our Nation's Capitol*. San Francisco, CA: HarperCollins, 2000.

Peterson, Scott. *Native American Prophecies*. New York: Paragon House, 1990.

Robbins, Tom. *Jitterbug Perfume*. New York: Bantam Books, 1984.

Sams, Jamie. *Sacred Path Cards*. HarperSanFrancisco, 1990.

Schaff, Gregory. *Wampum Belts and Peace Trees: George Morgan, Native Americans and Revolutionary Diplomacy*. Golden, CO: Fulcrum Publishing, 1990.

Shearer, Tony. *Beneath the Moon and Under the Sun: A Reappraisal of the Sacred Calendar and the Prophecies of Ancient Mexico*. Santa Fe, NM: Sun Publishing Co., 1975.

Shearer, Tony. *Lord of the Dawn, Quetzalcoatl: Great Prophecies of Ancient Mexico*. Happy Camp, CA: Naturegraph Publishers, Inc., 1971.

Snyder, Gary. *Turtle Island*. New York: New Directions Books, 1969.

Sun Bear and Wabun Wind. *Black Dawn, Bright Day*. Spokane, WA: Bear Tribe Publishing, 1990.

Thompson, William Irwin. *Blue Jade from the Morning Star: An Essay and a Cycle of Poems on Quetzalcoatl*. West Stockbridge, MA: The Lindisfarne Press, 1983

Trungpa, Chögyam. *Shambhala: The Sacred Path of the Warrior.* Boston, MA: Shambhala Publications, 1984.

Waters, Frank. *The Book of the Hopi.* Middlesex, England: Penguin Books, 1963.

Williams, Anne Richardson. *Unconventional Means: The Dream Down Under (with Aboriginal Traditional Stories as told by Lorraine Mafi–Williams).* In Circle Press, Nashville, TN, 2000),

Willoya, William, and Vinson Brown. *Warriors of the Rainbow: Strange and Prophetic Dreams of the Indian Peoples.* Happy Camp, CA: Naturegraph Publishers, 1962.

Wilson, James. *The Earth Shall Weep: A History of Native America.* New York, NY: Grove Press, 1998.

Ywahoo, Dhyani. *Voices of Our Ancestors: Cherokee Teachings from the Wisdom Fire.* Boston, MA: Shambhala Publications, Inc., 1987.

About the Author

Steven McFadden is director of Chiron Communications. A widely traveled journalist, teacher and healer, he is also the author of several books, including:

Profiles in Wisdom: Native Elders Speak About the Earth (iUniverse.com, 2000)

Farms of Tomorrow: Community Supported Farms, and Farm Supported Communities (Biodynamic Farming and Gardening Assoc., 1998, with Trauger Groh)

Teach Us To Number Our Days (Element Books, Ltd., 1996)

The Little Book of Native American Wisdom (Element Books Ltd, 1994)

Steven has been a practitioner of a healing art called Reiki since 1978, and a Reiki Master since 1990. He assisted John Harvey Gray and Lourdes Gray in writing their book, *Hand to Hand: The Longest Practicing Reiki Master Tells His Story* (Xlibris.com 2001).

You may contact the author through:

CHIRON COMMUNICATIONS
7 Avenida Vista Grande #195
Santa Fe, NM 87505-9199
www.chiron–communications.com

How to Order Books by Steven McFadden

Profiles in Wisdom: Native Elders Speak About the Earth

Taking a lead from John F. Kennedy's Pulitzer Prize winning *Profiles in Courage,* journalist Steven McFadden presents the stories and thinking of 17 contemporary Native American spiritual teachers. This is a fascinating and eclectic group of men and women, each with a passionate vision of spirituality based on the concepts of respect, balance, and harmony found in Native American traditions. Their deeply intelligent ideas radiate compassion and insight.

Published by iUniverse.com ISBN 0-595-14484-5
Order from www.Amazon.com or call 1-877-823-9235

Farms of Tomorrow Revisited:
Community Supported Farms, Farm Supported Communities
BY TRAUGER GROH AND STEVEN MCFADDEN

Family farms have collapsed by the thousands in recent decades in the face of competition from huge corporate industrial farms, and the onslaught of genetically engineered food. Yet, while this has happened, ordinary families in hundreds of American towns, villages, and cities have established and supported communty farms. These farms produce clean, healthy food that is grown and then eaten locally. The farms serve as environmental oases for the communities where they are located, and they provide dignified work in nature that heals, rather than harms, the earth. *Farms of Tomorrow Revisited* is the definitive text on this crucial subject. This book is not just for farmers, but for everyone who eats.

Published by the Biodynamic Assoc. ISBN 0-938-25013-2
Order from www.Amazon.com or call toll-free: 1-888-516-7797

Visit the Chiron Communications web site,
where all of Steven McFadden's books are available:

CHIRON COMMUNICATIONS
7 Avenida Vista Grande #195
Santa Fe, NM 87505-9199
www.chiron-communications.com